Where Asphalt Ends

Sketches from a Door County Summer Childhood

Corinne Bliss Livesay

with illustrations by the author

Beaver's Pond Press, Inc.
Edina, Minnesota

ISBN 1-931646-14-7

Library of Congress Catalog Number: 2001095139

Printed in the United States of America.

04 03 02 01 6 5 4 3 2

Beaver's Pond Press, Inc.

5125 Danen's Drive
Edina, Minnesota 55439-1465
(952) 829-8818
www.beaverspondpress.com

Dedication

to my mother, Nellie Dickerson;
Anne, Mary, and Helen Walton;
"The Oshkoshers;" the Floyd Knudsons;
family and friends who helped in the editing of this book
and Ephraim, a gift to children.

Table of Contents

Prologue

FOR THOSE INTERESTED IN THE BACKGROUND OF THIS BOOK, it is important to note that these stories were not written as historical accounts. Instead, they are memories, and I have tried to arrange the essays in chronological order where possible. And, for those who wish to know my exact age when some of the events occurred, a specific age is difficult to pinpoint now and not necessarily important. Growing up is a process divided more by stages and marked by events rather than by years.

I have been reminded that in the 1930s and '40s, an asphalt, not a gravel road, extended all the way from Sturgeon Bay to Gills Rock. True. It did, though most of the side roads were gravel ones. I even recall once riding on a "corduroy" road, one of closely laid parallel logs covered with crushed rock. However, the title of this book, *Where Asphalt Ends*, has little to do with any specific road. "Asphalt" is a metaphor instead.

Taking side roads stimulate one's sense of curiosity, and exploring gravel roads by car became a summer pastime. Gravel roads led to unexpected places, often to nowhere—the pinnacle of all destinations! And that is what childhood craves; not the convenient, purposeful and predictable places adults are prone to choose in their maturity, but those places where adventure, exploration, surprise and wonder begin. The village of Ephraim was my gravel road, and the most exciting portion of my formative childhood began there each summer. But, those greatest of all adventures a child can have were made possible by the somewhat inadvertent gifts given by three devoted maiden aunties, who shared themselves completely, unstintingly and in unbelievable abundance. In the end, it was they who made such a childhood as mine possible and this book is, in good part, a tribute to them, my role models of commitment.

For readers who are Ephraim, Wisconsin, or Door County buffs, about 1933, when I was two, my parents experienced their first vacation there. Both my mother and my aunts spent two weeks together at Edgewater Lodge where some of my earliest memories began. Later, my aunts rented one of Mrs. Barnes' cabins on the shore for a month each summer, which my mother and I shared with them for one or two weeks. Later, they rented a house at the top of what as children we called the Big Hill on Q, and where I, initially, spent part of, and, finally, the entire summers with them. Eventually, they purchased a house of their own closer to the village on Q when they decided to extend their vacation from May through October.

In the end, my mother bought her own small, original log cabin, which she sold several years after I was married in 1961 and had moved to White Bear Lake, Minnesota. Once my children arrived, the distance to Ephraim was too great, and with a large old house, gardens and pets, there was little time for extended vacations. But, I felt compelled to direct my own children and as many of their young friends as I could gather, to wander down those exciting, unpredictable gravel roads of childhood, just as I had been so fortunate to do.

Corinne B. Livesay

Introduction

If there is truth in the idea that some things assume lives of their own, it has been so in the writing of this book. What began as a characterization of a specific village and those who lived there also became a lament over today's loss of community and of an amiable, gracious way of life. Those who still do or have ever lived in a small town will most likely recall experiences and individuals easily substituted for those presented here.

Because this is a selection of summer recollections before and during World War II, it is, in part, historical. It is also about a childhood not in any way comparable to one today. During those years, few mothers worked, and with the exception of Bisquick, most meals were made from scratch. The responsibility of caring for children was everybody's business. As a result, parents were less apprehensive about their offspring's safety: exploration and wandering on one's own was one of the rights of childhood. However, the watershed experience of World War II and its aftermath reshaped America's collective self-consciousness and rapidly changed realities and behaviors from that time on. Those still living who were a part of that era have shaped, and still are shaping, who we are as a people today.

New affluence, increased mobility and advancing technologies following The War were contributing factors in the subtle transformation of our lives. Our habit had been to read books, play games, sing songs, hold deep dinner conversations, picnic and walk together. TV had not yet been invented, and gasoline was scarce. The professor, physician, grocer, plumber and auto mechanic were respected friends and neighbors, each integral to one's individual well-being and, consequently, to the entire community.

Although many remember the small communities in which they grew up as petty-minded places they couldn't wait to leave, Ephraim in Door County, Wisconsin, has always lured back both young and old. Weary of urban stresses, many Americans are now returning to small towns as worthy places in which to raise families and to retire. They are seen as places where people still share neighborly concern, where doors often remain unlocked, and individualism and eccentricity are colorful marks of character as much as they are flaws. The delight so many people take in Garrison Keillor's stories of Lake Wobegone, its Norwegian bachelor farmers, and the Side Track Tap, may indicate some deep-seated human need for the benediction of small, uncomplicated places. Perhaps we are analogous to pigeons flying home.

My vacations were certainly privileged ones, even for those times. I was aware of that and more than grateful for it. Both winter and summer residents were very dependent upon each other's talents and labors from May through October, which made Ephraim, for me and certainly for others, an ideal community of a sort few could imagine. Short- and long-time vacationers retreated there to find refreshment and renewal amid unparalleled scenery. At the same time, they found release in the quiet, unaffected lifestyle and comfort in shared interests and values. The result was enduring common bonds.

CBL

The author, with one of the last Captains of a steamer in Eagle Harbor, circa 1936

Aunt Anne, Aunt Helen and Aunt Mary with Corinne at the lakeshore in front of the Edgewater Hotel, Ephraim, Wisconsin, about 1935

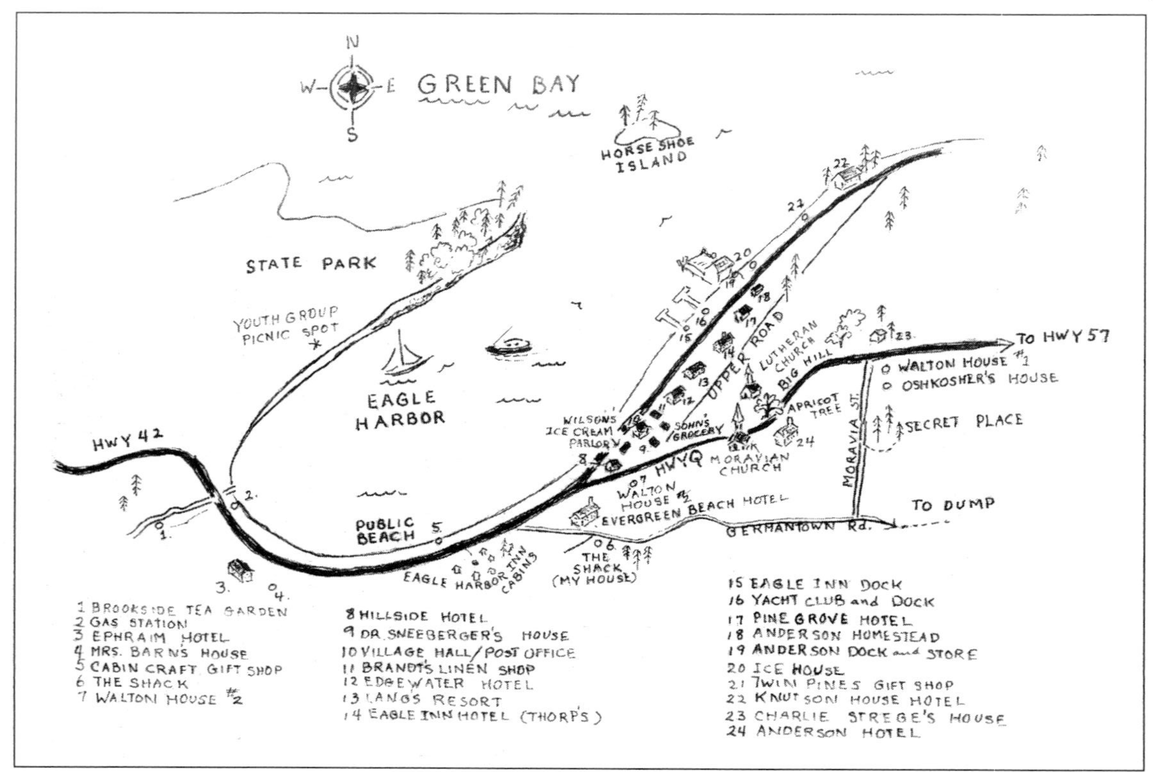
N
W
E
S
GREEN BAY
HORSE SHOE ISLAND
STATE PARK
YOUTH GROUP PICNIC SPOT
EAGLE HARBOR
HWY 42
PUBLIC BEACH
EAGLE HARBOR INN CABINS
THE SHACK (MY HOUSE)
WILSONS ICE CREAM PARLOR
SOHN'S GROCERY
HWY Q
WALTON HOUSE #2
EVERGREEN BEACH HOTEL
GERMANTOWN Rd.
MORAVIAN CHURCH
UPPER ROAD
LUTHERAN CHURCH
BIG HILL
APRICOT TREE
MORAVIA ST.
TO HWY 57
WALTON HOUSE #1
OSHKOSHER'S HOUSE
SECRET PLACE
TO DUMP
1 BROOKSIDE TEA GARDEN
2 GAS STATION
3 EPHRAIM HOTEL
4 MRS. BARNS HOUSE
5 CABIN CRAFT GIFT SHOP
6 THE SHACK
7 WALTON HOUSE #2
8 HILLSIDE HOTEL
9 DR. SNEEBERGER'S HOUSE
10 VILLAGE HALL/POST OFFICE
11 BRANDT'S LINEN SHOP
12 EDGEWATER HOTEL
13 LANGS RESORT
14 EAGLE INN HOTEL (THORP'S)
15 EAGLE INN DOCK
16 YACHT CLUB and DOCK
17 PINE GROVE HOTEL
18 ANDERSON HOMESTEAD
19 ANDERSON DOCK and STORE
20 ICE HOUSE
21 TWIN PINES GIFT SHOP
22 KNUTSON HOUSE HOTEL
23 CHARLIE STREGE'S HOUSE
24 ANDERSON HOTEL

As It Was

EPHRAIM, WISCONSIN, IN THE 1930S AND 1940S WAS TO MOST summer visitors a compellingly picturesque fishing village with a small residential population that couldn't have exceeded more than three hundred. But as early as the late 1800s, however, its pristine charm and rugged natural beauty, chronicled and extolled by explorers, missionaries and early settlers, had made it a magnet for tourists and summer residents. Relatively accessible by steamer and stagecoach from cities such as Milwaukee and Chicago, it was a mecca for those who craved relief from the the city's searing summer heat.

Here was offered a landscape of such enormous proportions as to place the most grandiose of human endeavors into proper perspective. In short, it was another world. The narrow peninsula with its rocky, irregular shorelines juts approximately sixty miles into Lake Michigan and creates an area of the lake called Green Bay. At the end of the peninsula lies a treacherous strait called Death's Door from which Door County derived its name.

So wild and craggy were the cliffs and bluffs, so snug the harbor, so plentiful the whitefish and trout in those early days, that the immigrant Norwegians who first settled there found the landscape a counterpart to the fjords they had left back home. They logged and fished, utilized their seafaring skills against the savage short swells of Green Bay and Lake Michigan, and pitted their tenacity and physical endurance against harsh winters and unyielding, rocky fields.

The configuration of Ephraim can be imagined like the letter J with the left hook extended a bit. Each side of the J should be visualized as massive bluffs with Eagle Harbor in the middle. Beyond the open ends of the J lie the expansive waters of Green Bay. A single road dives from the left or west peninsula to the harbor and village below, hugging the shoreline of the little bay and serving as the main thoroughfare through town. Several side roads join it as it curves along an eastern bluff.

Only one is of any importance to the village, strung out along the shore: County Trunk Q, which ascends the bluff at an angle halfway through town. It reaches a narrow plateau midway up the hill before dividing like a Y. A small branch, The Upper Road, parallels the road below and soon joins it to the north. But Q suddenly hairpins east at what seems a forty-five degree angle, snakes to the summit of the bluff, and crosscuts to the Lake Michigan side of the peninsula. This eastern bluff, against which the town is built, is gentler than the one on the western side of the harbor, and instead of making a sheer rise from the lake, it begins its ascent about seven hundred yards from the water's edge.

Childhood's uncluttered and impressionable mind files new experiences like colored snapshots in photo albumns; indelible and permanent. They become realities which often surface thereafter, floating between the past and present tense. I, for example, even at age four and five, recalled ten hotels facing the bay, nine scattered along the road through town and one high on the bluff where Q and the upper road diverge. They were wide, white, two- to three-storied buildings with red or green roofs and broad pillared porches, and most had sweeping front yards complimented with horseshoe pits and shuffleboard courts.

Beside hotels, the following establishments circle the shore at the bottom of the hill, approaching from the west: a bakery with an accompanying restaurant, a small gas station, several small rental cottages, an ice cream parlor, the Village Hall and post office, two docks, (one belonging to the yacht club) the notable Anderson Dock with large accompanying boathouse and small grocery, an ice house, and finally another gift shop farther up the road.

The village proper terminated at its northern end with one last hotel. There, the road began to rise again, and continued in a roller coaster-fashion to the tip of the peninsula. Several houses, another hotel and two church steeples rose against the bluff above and behind the Village Hall. They were white intrusions among the dark cedars, maples and pines clinging to the cliff face.

Brookside Tea Garden was a restaurant and bakery set in the woods near the beginning of the south end of town. The aroma of Hilda's homemade rolls, breads and pastries permeated the air nearly to the main road. In the small attached dining room, meals of gourmet quality often began with cold strawberry or cucumber soup and might end with four-inch-high slices of baked Alaska pie. The tiny dining room overlooked a little stream stained brown with tannin from the dense cedar swamp behind it.

Within several yards, the little brook ran under the highway, emerged on the other side and flowed into the bay, adjacent to the cement apron of a small gas station specializing in general car repair. There were several cabins north of the station, followed by the public beach, more cabins and then the Cabin Craft Gift Shop, run by Doris Heizie. Doris, who lived in her shop, and combined her entrepreneurial and artistic skills, crafting customized silver jewelry and pewter plates. From there on, there was little on the bay side of the highway except rocks and sand.

Roughly in the village center, just before the Village Hall, was Wilson's Ice Cream Parlor. It was always busy. Mr. Wilson carried a good selection of sunglasses, souvenirs, post cards and cigars. Nearly every afternoon, the parlor was filled with teenagers squandering their allowances on chocolate Cokes, hot fudge sundaes and banana splits. Hunger was the girls' excuse for hanging out and meeting boys. Girls of summer spent a good deal of time there in the first flushes of puberty, giggling obstreperously, booth hopping and playing the juke box.

About a block up a short side road by the Village Hall was Sohn's Grocery, the only local store we patronized for groceries and meat. Their major offerings were selections of canned goods, shampoo, sundries, a modicum of local vegetables and, occasionally, fresh fruit. Refrigerated trucks were not common yet. Perishable items were rare and arrived, if at all, about once a week. Across the road from the grocery was Brandt's Linen Shop, whose tables, drawers and walls groaned under the weight of fine imported tablecloths, towels decorated with silk screened calendars and woodland scenes, and beautifully embroidered handkerchiefs, many too elegant for general use. Well-to-do repeat vacationers anticipated Mr. Brandt's newly stocked selections each summer until several years after the war when life became more casual. Place mats gradually supplanted tablecloths, paper substituted for decorative linen towels, and Kleenex made hankies nearly obsolete.

A short distance beyond the yacht club and its accompanying docks was the Anderson homestead and tiny quick-stop grocery, the latter on the lake side of the road. Several yards below the store, a huge dock accommodating a barn-sized boathouse dominated the landscape. Until the middle '30s, it berthed Goodrich steamers and brought tourists and supplies to the community. Later, it was used by commercial fishermen for unloading, cleaning and packing their catch, and by recreational yachtsmen. They frequently docked for several days to rest or to replenish supplies at the conveniently located general store, whose perishables consisted mostly of milk, eggs and, occasionally, local seasonal fruits and vegetables.

Mr. Adolf Anderson and family, owners of both dock and store, always wore a white shirt and a black yachting cap. He had two sisters: Miss Munda, who was never seen without a blue ribbon in her white hair and Miss Lizzie, whose hair bore a pink one. Mr. Anderson stocked items in his store he assumed boaters needed, though not necessarily more upscale items customers and boaters asked for; and those not familiar with the family's quirks were frequently put off by their sternness and rigidity.

Additionally, the store carried such basics as underwear, socks, and blue jeans, along with flannel and woolen shirts. But the stock moved slowly. Old high-button shoes gathered dust on unreachable top shelves of the store. Candy bars were on the counter, but the line was drawn on the sale of chewing gum or tobacco.

Some thought Mr. Anderson had a take-it-or-leave-it attitude because he often took affront to criticism or suggestions about his store. If he didn't like someone, he or she knew it. He, along with his sisters, had a strict Moravian sense of what was and was not proper and never hesitated to share their morality with anyone they thought in need of hearing it. Still, all three had such sweet and honest natures, such resistance to worldliness and moral compromise, they were revered by the community—nearly, it seems, to the point of sanctification.

A large wooden ice house a few feet north of the store, provided ice for packing whitefish and lake trout, as well as for the ice boxes in hotels, homes and cottages. Large translucent ice blocks were stacked ten or more high and smothered in wet insulating sawdust. There was always concern about running short of ice if the weather were warm. Although most vacationers from the city had electric refrigerators at home, power up and down the the peninsula was undependable, especially during nasty storms. After struggling with the chunks of ice melting in their lead-lined wooden ice box for a number of summers, my aunts (whom I shall refer to collectively as "Auntie Waltons" in the future), decided to purchase a gas refrigerator that was not dependent on the vagaries of the power company. It was illogical to me however, that a gas flame could provide refrigeration on the one hand and heat to the oven on the other!

The last small establishment in town was Mrs. Matter's Twin Pines Antique Shop. Set in a damp tangle of dark cedars, it was a literal museum containing one of the most impressive antique collections in the Midwest. Rooms were jammed from top to bottom with Crown Darby teapots, Delft, Dutch silver from early New Amsterdam, 16th-century hand-colored Mercator maps, rare tin plates, and every sort of glass and furniture imaginable. It was a storybook cottage. The green shutters were ornamented with pine tree cutouts, and a tinkling bell over the doorway announced customers. On rainy days when the Franklin stove was lit to warm the clammy four rooms upstairs and the living quarters below, the entire shop smelled like pine, wood smoke and old store rooms.

Summer in the village was so uncomplicated and unsophisticated, that the simplest occurrences and minute observations became a reason for excitement. That was evident even in the furniture found in many cottages, replaced in the succeeding years by those who favored either more practical pieces or chose to display their affluence with trendier styles. Chairs were made from rough pine and cedar logs, and desk drawer fronts were of halved logs riddled with the trackings of worms. My eyes traced the worm hole mazes by the hour, and I wondered if these desks were fashioned from ancient trees dredged up from the bottom of Green Bay by some wild storm. How wonderful to have crafted something so beguiling! Pillows stuffed with aromatic balsam needles graced cottage sofas like lavender sachets snuggled into dresser drawers. In winter, their woodsy fragrance recalled summer, especially if the weather were damp and the needles crushed.

Few sounds were heard except for boat motors, an occasional car, a few voices, and waves on the beach mingling with the wind and the rustling of maples and pines. There were wild days and wild nights when waves mounted with ever-increasing metronomical thunder upon the shore. Days followed when water in the harbor, and beyond, was a still sheet of blue shimmering glass. July brought many days of heavy rain or brooding mist and fog so thick that landscape details were shrouded or obscured. Ensuing days might have been of absolute clarity and skin-fondling silky soft breezes. Deep involuntary breaths sucked up the clean-sheet smell of ozone and the saltless sea to the north.

There was a pervasive odor of living water and wet rocks mingled with damp tree bark and sweet vegetation from the woods. These were the earthy, sensory connections which compelled one to set aside all thoughts beyond the moment and threaded one into primitive, uncomplicated sleep. Unfortunately, it was a sleep that marked one more day from the all-too-brief calendar of summer.

A second ago is technically history, though we perceive it as part of present experience. This is true of the people, situations and experiences here, and will be, as long as anyone can read or remember. Ephraim in the period of limited tourist discovery seemed a nearly idyllic place. Of course, everyone understands no town is perfect: towns are reflections of ourselves. But fortunately, children remember only the best, and when they are inspired by beauty and shaped by exceptional adults and acquaintances, they can overcome unpleasantness more easily. For anyone who has grown up in a small community, theirs may be, as this one still is for me, the most perfect and important place; memorable and always present.

The Going

EACH SPRING IN EARLY JUNE AFTER SCHOOL FINISHED, THE green Chrysler I had anticipated minute by minute since 5:30 would at last round the corner of our block and pull up in front of the house around 6:00 A.M. Aunt Helen, driver and organizer, and one of my three "love aunts" as opposed to an actual relative, would open the car trunk and begin rearranging everything to accommodate my two allotted suitcases, fishing pole, tackle box, bug book, crayons, etc. Of course, there was always more, which was stuffed into nooks and crannies and tunneled into any available black hole.

The packing always made Aunt Helen irritable, even more so if Aunt Anne tried to tell her just how she would do it to make things fit. The driver always had to do it her way. Aunt Mary would chide me for always bringing too much stuff, and Aunt Anne would tell the other two that she didn't mind riding with the extras in the back seat. There would be grumbling about the picnic basket being back there also, and that others who sat there might want a little leg room, even if she didn't. Eventually, controversies were settled, some things had to be carted from the sidewalk back up to my bedroom, Mother kissed me goodbye, and the four of us pulled out of Rockford, Illinois, at the usual time, 6:30 in the morning.

"IF YOU
DON'T KNOW
WHOSE SIGNS
THESE ARE
YOU CAN'T HAVE DRIVEN
VERY FAR.
BURMA SHAVE."

We craned our necks to read those entertaining signs strung along the narrow blacktop roads that led to summer. Beloit, Janesville, Ft. Atkinson, home of Freeman Shoes. Then came Watertown, Juneau. At Waupun, not quite halfway, we pulled into a small park in the center of a residential area of the town. It was circular, and small houses faced it all around. There was a little well-maintained municipal garden, a water spigot and a picnic table. Across the street was the single-pump station where Aunt Helen ritually refilled the car with gasoline and we used the toilet. We stopped there because the station owner was so accommodating and friendly, remembering us from year to year. This was the familiar commons where we parked around 10:00 A.M., stretched our legs and ate the lunch packed by Aunt Mary. Now, it seemed, we were really on our way. Halfway. Too far to turn back. Refreshed, we rearranged our seating in the car and started out again.

We rolled past little farm towns, yellow-eared hybrid corn signs, barns decorated with tobacco advertising.

"THE CHICK, HE WED, LET OUT A WHOOP,
FELT HIS CHIN AND, FLEW THE COOP."

"Let's play, Animal, Vegetable or Mineral. You go first."
"All right, I'm thinking of something."
"Is it Animal?"

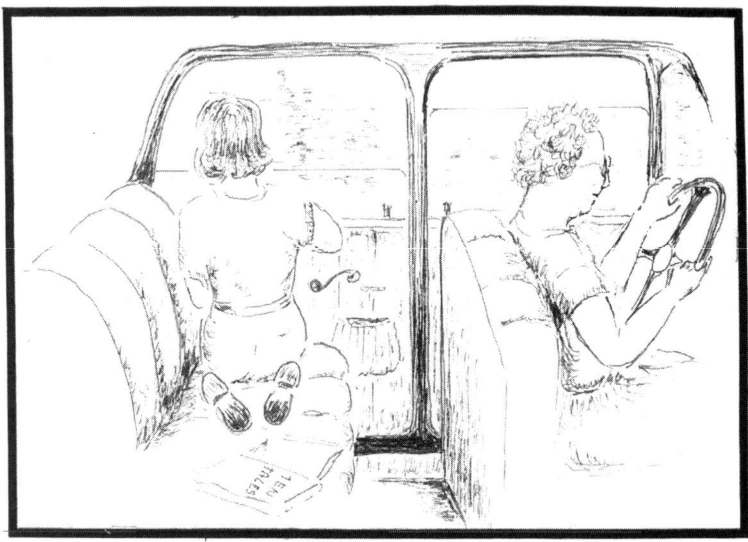

"No."

"Is it Vegetable?"

"Yes."

"Is it bigger than a bread box?"

Fond du lac. Diocese of Fond du lac. Catholics, churches and more churches. Each town presents its special flavor. Names on storefronts mark immigrants' trails. History on wheels. Gardens of pink poppies. Bohemia and sweet kolacky buns. "How long until we get there?" Down the hill into De Pere, a comfortable city, as if settled in an easy chair. More hard maples now than oaks. "How far to Green Bay?" Sing. Sing from the *Golden Book*, all the rounds. "Let's do it again and I'll start last. Now let's do 'Solomon Levi!'" Sing. Sing them all. "I can't wait until we get there!"

"Count bars then," my aunts would say. "That will keep you busy." Into Green Bay, over the railroad tracks, over the, arched, rusty metal bridge and into the city. Turn to the left. The Hotel Swoboda, and Prange's Department Store to the right where, last year, Aunt Mary bought our summer dishes.

Dykesville. Brussels and the little shrine still standing in a farmer's field. Tornado Alley. The great Peshtigo forest fire, the Indian massacre. "How much longer?" Down the big hill into Sturgeon Bay, the lake ahead, breath of the peninsula. Gulls, smells of fish and smoking chubs. Over the bridge where nonchalant gulls perch on railing posts. Open the windows wider, poke my head out. Draw in the heady odor of morning catch and sublimed gasoline. Hulk of a freighter to the left, half done in the shipyard. Schooner and ketch full-sailed to the right, cruisers bobbing in their slips close by the bridge. Sailors in bell bottoms on sidewalks, smart-looking, white-capped and handsome. Oh, just to be one!

Stop at the grocery near the end of town for stocking empty cupboards and refrigerator. I can't wait another minute. Can't they shop faster? But, there is much to buy. We've been on the road for nearly seven hours! At last, we straddle the sacks of groceries at our feet and ascend the steep hill with the sharp turn at the top. Another stop. Fill the car again with gas, buy ice cream cones.

"Shall we take Highway 57 or 42?" Make a decision. The Michigan or the Bay side? It was 42 we took last year.

"57," we agree.

"When we drive home then, we'll take 42."

"I can't wait to smell it," I proclaim. "That smell of Lake Michigan air! How much longer do you think it'll be? Half hour? An hour?" We all count taverns by the roadside to make the time go faster.

"Look. There's a freighter out there. See? Wa-a-ay out on the horizon?" We're entering the other world now. Historical marker. Pére Marquette. Nicolet. But, no time to stop for lookouts.

"Smell the pine? Smell the wood stoves burning? Smell kerosene stoves!" Open the windows. Let the wind blow hair. My, how Lake Michigan transforms the air. "Smell Ephraim? I do." It's all familiar now, each house by the side of the road, each decorative windmill in a yard, each log cabin, tumbling stone and timber barn, each old windswept pine still bent the same as last year—to the west. Breathe it all in; fresh rolling waves, coolness of late spring and balsam woods. I cannot breathe enough.

Closer. Thoughts of familiar places awaiting within a few short miles unite us: the limestone walls ringing the gardens of the front yard, the light-dappling birches and maples near the back screen door, the fieldstone fireplace in the comfortable west-facing living room with ordered window view of meadow, rail fence, steeple, bay and distant bluff. The everpresent pine scent from the paneling of the breakfast room. Oriental rugs and antiques brought from home, though out of keeping with a summer house, will still provide a feeling of welcome and comfort. Aunt Helen's hands relax upon the steering wheel, Aunt Anne plans her garden and Aunt Mary, evening supper. I plan rediscovery. Inexplicably, there seems little need to hurry now, the certainty of home suddenly peacefully and happily sufficient.

Bells

BELLS OFFERED A PATTERN TO OUR SUMMER DAYS AND SEPARATED mornings from the afternoons and evenings. Ten hotels had ten distinctly different bells whose tones resounded daily throughout the village. Like churches announcing daily offices, they called eager guests to breakfast, lunch and dinner. Waitresses coursed hotel grounds and porches like school marms clanging children to classes. At other hotels, discarded school or ship bells creaked and groaned on ungreased brackets mounted on exterior walls near hotel kitchens. And, if the wind was from the north, the sonorous reverberation of the largest hotel bell, mingled its music with the others. Their varied pitches drifted through the air from one end of the village to the other and were as identifiable as voices. Any one bell failing to ring within ten or fifteen minutes of the others meant something had gone wrong in that particular hotel kitchen.

If there were a beginning or an end to the village, it was the bells that parenthesized it, from Knudson House at the north to Hotel Ephraim at the south. For children, those sounds established a boundary beyond which there was little reason to venture: they were the beginning and the end of the summer world in which we lived. Watches were unnecessary. When the lunch or supper bell rang, the longest walk along the road to home took no more than twenty minutes.

Sometimes, before 6:00 A.M., I dressed soundlessly, eased the screen door nearly to its squeak, and slipped into the morning where sounds were uncluttered and precise. Gravel sliding under tennis shoes, voices from a hotel kitchen, bird calls, all seemed to be cut from paper, singular and present only for me, the listener. In still, damp morning air, smells of kerosene and wood smoke hung low like haze under trees, mingling with cedar and the sweet pungency of sausage cooking.

At the shore, small boats bobbed quietly, ropes loosening with the swells, then pulling taut against their moorings. From the inside of boat cabins, one might hear muffled voices and elbows bumping bulkheads as sleepy occupants dressed in cramped quarters. I could hear the dull clatter of breakfast dishes and catch the smell of coffee being brewed and bacon frying. A cabin hatch would suddenly open and a yachtsman would emerge with a yawn and a prolonged indulgent stretch, scanning the sky in a brief assessment of the weather. Soon, an extended hand would appear from below to offer a steaming mug through the open hatch. Easing into a deck chair and claiming the morning for his very own, the satisfied sojourner would contentedly sip coffee from the deck of his "little piece of heaven." Boaters did their best to ignore early morning gawkers such as I.

"Hi there," I'd say, even if no one was looking in my direction. "Are you going to sail today? Are you spending the week here? Gee, I bet it's neat sleeping on a boat. Do ya ever get seasick at night from all that rocking? Where's your boat from? Where else are you going? Do you ever fish off your boat? Is your galley big enough to cook a dinner in?" All these questions were ploys to provoke conversation. "I live here all summer. We own a cottage," I'd tell them, hoping they'd be impressed with the fact that though they might have a boat, we had an entire house!

If I were lucky, they might say, "Hi," in return or, "We don't cook much on the boat." But usually they'd concentrate once more on their coffee, figuring indifference was the best method of curing pesky people. Any further chitchat on my part was usually ignored, and when the breakfast bells rang, I had an excuse to terminate the one-sided conversation on my own terms. "Guess I'd better head home for breakfast," I'd remark and, with a confident wave and goodbye, saunter home, pretending I hadn't been thoroughly snubbed. If I rented a row boat later in the morning to fish or to explore the shoreline, lunch bells warned me to hurry in to avoid paying an extra quarter for another hour. Besides, fish don't bite well at noon.

If I explored the woods instead, "bell time" prompted searching for the flattest rock slab on which to spread my carefully prepared sack lunch. In that marvelous isolation, I munched on carrot sticks, tried to understand the meaning of life or surmised that the bread, which had been rising when I left the house, was more than likely done, still warm enough to melt the butter.

Late in the afternoon, guests gathered on hotel porches. They discussed the previous evening's spectacular sunset or made plans for afterdinner card games. Often a celebrated musician would perform an informal evening concert in the hotel living room. Guests debated how far they could walk after supper and still be back in time to hear it. The rockers strung across front porches soon filled with waiting diners, though the most anxious stood in clusters close to dining room entrances.

While any clothing, no matter how ragged or soiled, was appropriate during the day, one was expected to dress respectably for a hotel dinner. A well-known person or an intellectual might be seated with you at the table, and a defining first impression was important. Ladies wore silk or cotton dresses, necklaces and earrings. Garden flowers were placed in the center of each table, and even the breakfast tables were set with white cloths and napkins. Regular guests were given the same seating arrangement throughout their stay. That way, waitresses could more easily respond to idiosyncrasies.

Sometimes this worked out well, and lasting friendships between diners were cemented through year after year of sharing three meals each day for a week or two. Many people timed their following year's vacation with that of a newfound friend. But occasionally, the consequences were disastrous. A really difficult or irritating woman who could barely be tolerated by those sitting with her presented a dilemma, as asking to be seated at a different table could initiate a chain of unpleasant circumstances. Moving from one table to another, especially if the hotel were completely booked, upset more than one group of guests. The culprit, usually overly talkative, highly opinionated, or of a self-righteous nature, spent remaining mealtimes in such a bitter and defensive state that the others simply endured mealtime in relatively sullen silence. There was a distinct sigh of relief from everyone when that guest's stay was over and life returned to normal, particularly from the viewpoint of the hotel owner, whose duty was to keep everybody happy!

"You've simply *got* to seat us at another table. I just cannot endure another meal with that woman!" I recall one guest saying to the owner, as in complete frustration, she jiggled tense hands and fists at the side of her bosom. "If I have to sit with her again, I'm going home tomorrow. She's practically ruined my entire vacation!"

There was no doubt that seating arrangements were a gamble, and no matter how carefully the management tried to guess who might get along with whom at mealtime, the possibility remained of being stuck at a table with a terrible bore on the one hand, or a cantankerous blabbermouth on the other. If anything hastened the end of the American Plan at summer hotels across the country, (a rate that included a room plus three meals a day) seating arrangements such as these had to be a partial cause.

Fridays were always fish days and chicken was served at nearly every hotel on Sunday. Each place was noted for something it prepared especially well. Good cooking and thoughtful proprietors seemed more important than the appointments in the room where one slept. Guests lodged at their preferred hotel became so loyal to it over the years that critical comparisons to other inns were taken as near-personal insults. Strong allegiances were formed through food, cards and conversation, and devoted visitors returned year after year. When they became too old to travel alone, the elders often came, cane in hand, accompanied by their own aging children.

The bell that rang for dinner was the final accent to the day and established the social tenor of the evening. About every other week, my aunts treated themselves to a hotel dinner, and we all looked forward to it. The smells of good cooking while waiting for the bell to ring whetted the appetite and made stomachs yearn for satisfaction. There was visiting and laughter, and the entire event seemed as much a party as a dinner out.

Just as exciting as the eating was to talk with people who lived in cities I had never visited or who came from countries worlds away and seemed to lead lives much more interesting than those of anyone else I knew. Most days, however, scents escaping from hot hotel kitchens, the sight of empty porches, and the sound of bells drew me up the hill toward home. Those signals were the assurance that I would be on time for a supper in the dining room with Auntie Waltons. Though we were all on summer vacation, mealtime was still an important ritual, and they expected me to be there on time.

The bells were removed several decades ago. Hotels were remodeled and stopped serving meals. I can hardly blame them, as the work was Herculean. Restaurants have replaced them, but the shape of our lives and the character of the village was altered in the change. The warm social fabric woven by summer guests who shared sunsets, stuffed themselves on chicken dinners and cherry pies, and visited around hotel living room fireplaces faded also.

There was great comfort afforded by those bells. They structured time without the constraint of hours and minutes; few have any idea how liberating that can be to both the body and to the spirit. For those who once lived by and can still recall their sounds, the air now seems empty, and somehow, strangely wrong; as if the atmosphere is waiting to be filled again with ringing.

The Walton Sisters

A PERFECT HOUSEHOLD MUST BE THE DULLEST PLACE ON EARTH, offering few challenges and little to recall. The Walton household was far from dull!

The Waltons were three unmarried sisters and long-time friends of my adoptive mother. We all lived in Rockford, Illinois, in the winter, and I felt their house was as much mine as theirs. Years later, I discovered they were aware of my background and were instrumental in the private adoption procedure. For that reason, they asked to be a part of my upbringing which turned out to be a fortunate arrangement, as Mother became a widow when I was eight. Suddenly forced to go to work, she had no idea how she could juggle her job and a child on summer vacation at the same time. Our two families had spent previous summer vacations together in Ephraim, first at Edgewater Lodge, and then at Mrs. Barnes' cottage on the bay. But Auntie Waltons decided to extend their vacation to five or six months and rented a large house at the top of the Big Hill. The move was just at the right time. They came to Mother's rescue, and mine, and I was theirs from the end of May until school started in September.

Fortunately, I was already used to their habits. Aunt Helen "hoiked" and cleared her throat in the morning, and Aunt Anne always drank juice or milk like a guppy. For that she was criticized unmercifully. A glass of juice for example, was held delicately. But as it approached her mouth, she would lock her lower lip firmly to the side of the glass and extend the upper one way over the rim like a fish, making noisy, hard, gulping sounds as she tipped the glass and her throat contracted around the liquid. It was marvelously entertaining to watch her do it.

Then there was the old two-sided flip toaster joyously acquired at a junk shop to replace the broken one. Toasting was a carefully monitored process. The slices were turned and reversed frequently, browned to crispy perfection, and dried to cacophonous crunchiness on the flat, shiny chrome toaster top. Our breakfasts were an orchestration of the earthiest form. "Anne!" the other two would rebuke with disgust, biting into their thin slices of Melba toast, "do you have to make those ridiculous noises every time you swallow?

As in any family, there are things one has to put up with. For me, my aunts' habit of using everything until there was nothing left to be gotten from it, as evidenced by their reuse of paper napkins and dusting paper, was my greatest irritant. Paper napkins were used for as long as a week at a time and were collected clockwise around the table after meals. Mine was on the bottom, then Aunt Anne's, (who had an egg every morning and whose napkin was therefore easily distinguishable) then Aunt Mary's, and finally, Aunt Helen's.

They were collected and dispensed in proper order ritualistically, even if there were company present, and I used to cringe when I set the table, feeling embarrassed for them as well as myself. How I wished I could crush those disgusting napkins up and toss them all away. "Waste not, want not," they said when I commented that they were soiled too badly for reuse, and after their careful examination, I usually had to set them out anyway. The same thing happened to the dusting paper used to wipe the wooden stairs. Dusting paper, a costly substitute for the rags vacationers had not had the chance to accumulate, came in a wax paper-like roll and could be torn off a sheet at a time. To earn my keep my duty was to clean the steps leading to the second-floor bedrooms at least once a week, and that paper had to be refolded a million times, it seemed, and then inspected before they finally approved the disposing of it. They were frugal and exceptional recyclers despite the fact that the era of the "disposable society" was well under way. The paper industry might now be close to bankruptcy if there had been many more like they. My mother said it came from their conservative English upbringing.

Aunt Helen was the decision maker, head of the household and chauffeur. The other two sisters acquiesced to her in all financial decisions, seldom questioning her authority on anything. Having been one of the chief accountants for Rockford Knitting Mills, she had developed a sound business head. It was she who decided which car to purchase, balanced the books, and worried until she broke out in hives over the ups and downs of the stock market.

Aunt Mary controlled household operations, and with Aunt Helen's occasional help, did most of the cooking. The two considered Anne an inept, fussbudgety nuisance in the kitchen, and they kept her out as much as possible. She was an artistic pianist and was told to stick to that. "If you cut your finger, you can't play!"

Aunt Anne took as much pride in her gardens as in her piano and organ playing and could give every plant its common and botanical name. Visitors came from all over to view her Hemerocallis and her extensive array of perennials in bloom. When she wasn't gardening or playing the piano, much of her summer was spent filling out memberships for the winter Community Concert Series she had been instrumental in bringing to our home town. (She was also president of The Rockford Mendelssohn Club) As a consequence of her dedication to what she called "good music" (which surprisingly included Benny Goodman) and because of several years of rigid classical education in Chicago, she never missed an opportunity to expose me to good music of every form. Like so many other members of the summer community she shared her talents, playing the organ in the Moravian Church on Sunday mornings and the piano at the Community Sing later in the evening.

Aunt Mary, the most delicate of the three, was tormented by hay fever and headaches, the latter presumably either migraines or the result of an illness contracted on a round-the-world tour in the 1920s. Like most women before the era of Kleenex, the three had accumulated stacks of miniature art works from Brandt's Linen Shop simply to catch sneezes. Aunt Mary's handkerchiefs were always close at hand, along with a bottle of Yardley's Lavender Smelling Salts, sniffed to revive herself from occasional fainting spells. Her headaches were frequently so intense that she sometimes went to bed for as long as a week and Aunt Anne was ordered not to practice the piano because it hurt Aunt Mary's head so much. I say ordered, because she was often treated as a child, her sisters telling her what she could or couldn't do. At times, she tried playing quietly anyhow, but the piano was right against the wall of Aunt Mary's bedroom and she was quickly warned to, "Stop it!"

Homemade bread was made each week, and in chilly weather, was placed over the hot air register to rise. Warm from the oven, the tender slices were spread with butter and homemade strawberry or raspberry jam, sending taste buds into such paroxysms of delight that an entire loaf could disappear in minutes. Dessert accompanied nearly every meal. When company came, they were elaborate, ranging from baked Alaska, floating islands, rum or brandy cakes, custards and tortes to a variety of homemade pies. Exciting cuisine was one of the summer's great advantages.

The Walton kitchen was also the stage for the weekly margarine toss. Margarine was illegally transported into what was known as "The Dairy State" each spring by hiding it among the blankets and pillows in the trunk of the car just in case of an accident involving the police. When margarine was first marketed, it was white, not yellow, and packaged like a butter block. Included was a small packet of red food dye for coloring. That was a messy process accomplished by blending the two in a bowl by hand. After The War, however, it was sealed in heavy-duty plastic bags with the bubble of food coloring conveniently enclosed. Each week according to turn, one of us stood in the center of the kitchen, gleefully squeezing and rupturing the bubble of dye and, fascinated, watched bursts of red and orange radiate into the snowy spread. Then the bag was thrown back and forth between us, each person giving it a quick kneading before tossing it on. We continued until our smuggled butter substitute was uniformly gold.

Most people can be defined by occupation and that was true of Auntie Waltons, whose avocations were highly cerebral. Rainy days were filled with a host of pleasures pursued. All three knit; during The War they turned out socks by the dozen (all made on small needles with fine yarn), lap warmers and long white bandages, which, together with the socks, were rolled up and sent off for needy soldiers. Date bars, because they stayed fresh so long, were frequently packaged and sent to Red Cross canteens as a welcome addition to doughnuts.

The aunties also made and designed their own clothes, usually in early spring before many summer friends arrived. It seemed the dining room table was always filled with material in the process of being cut. They also brought many hardcover crossword puzzle books with them to the cottage. Afternoons and evenings would be punctuated with, "What's a four letter word for money?", or, "What's a five letter word for a boat pole? Something, something, a, something, t." Aunt Anne did double cross sticks and anagrams and spent hours working on them. Aunt Mary, on the other hand, was addicted to mysteries. She read everything of Ellery Queen, Agatha Christie, Conan Doyle—any mystery on which she could get her hands. In the last years of her life, she had read them all and could find no new ones to her liking because not enough clues were given so she could solve the murder before the final chapter.

Conversations in their company were highlighted by series of quotations and stories. Though they had only a high school education, they could quote Shakespeare and tell tales of Greek gods and goddesses by the hour. They loved repeating a limerick about "Aphrodite without any nightie," just to hear me giggle. And, they were history buffs, expert at remembering dates of battles and stories of kings and queens. Sometimes, when there was a storm and candles were the only light we had, they'd take the part of Shakespeare's witches from *Macbeth*.

"When shall we meet again," one would say, "in thunder, lightning or rain?"

Aunt Mary would reply in a squeaky, high-pitched voice, "When the hurley burley's done."

"When the battle's lost and won," Aunt Anne would chortle evilly. Then they would laugh the witches' laugh and recite all the ingredients in the terrible brew.

Somewhere in the living room there was usually a card table set up for jigsaw puzzles, handmade wooden puzzles of card-table size and exasperating difficulty to assemble. We gathered to work on one as a family, moving the floor lamp as close to the table as possible, sorting pieces of similar shading and examining shapes and edges carefully. The more difficult they were to finish, the happier the aunties were, and sometimes it took more than a week for one to be completed. Various solitaires and bridge were other pastimes in addition to duplicate bridge. Many an afternoon I'd return from exploring to find the living room filled with ladies deep in a game or filling themselves with high-caloric desserts slathered in whipped cream.

Occasionally, sisterly disagreements degenerated into dandy arguments, usually at Aunt Anne's expense. The other two were capable of reducing her to tears, criticizing the way she held her hands, crossed her feet and drank her juice. They criticized her for taking opposite opinions to theirs.

"You certainly enjoy being contrary!" they'd nag. "Why

don't you try living in the real world for once!"

Sometimes they just didn't like the look on her face. When she fell into a pious or artistic mood, she would strike righteous poses, assuming the appearance of a visioned saint, entranced and haloed. It drove the other two quite mad to look at her. They would gang up on her and nothing that she did, or even who she was, pleased them. "Poor Aunt Anne," I'd say, "you're not nice to my Aunt Anne." I'd kiss her and try to make her feel better as the tears welled in her eyes and dribbled down her cheeks under her gold-rimmed glasses.

The adage "two is company and three is a crowd" likely applied to Auntie Waltons. Aunt Anne could be quite impractical, had a different temperament from the other two, and had always received special attention because of her artistic talent. I had the feeling she had always been an easy target for teasing. If I had had sisters or brothers of my own, perhaps I would have known that sibling rivalry doesn't abruptly end with childhood. As it was, I sided with Aunt Anne, the underdog, until the tension at last cleared.

Despite quirks and disagreements, theirs was a wonderful household, filled with poetry, music and creativity. When the bread rose, when the cookies came out of the oven, when Aunt Anne played the piano, or when they recalled episodes from trips around the world, I knew what a fortunate place it was for me, or any child, to be. With poor reception on the radio and little broadcast news available at the time, we were often cut off from the world except for books and the Sunday newspaper. Nevertheless, we entertained ourselves to the fullest. Their love of words and reading had taken them far beyond most college graduates of today. They were a family of scholars who consistently tried to convey a love of learning. In addition, it was a gracious home, frequently filled with house guests and friends who sought their company despite their-isms, even overlooking the paper napkins. (I imagine their house guests never again used one without recalling the penurious habit.)

My aunts were firm disciplinarians, but nevertheless, were

totally indulgent with their time; with simple, delightful surprises; and with affection. It was amazing how much three old maids without any experience in raising children had to give. They led very ordered lives and set specific rules and boundaries for me. At the same time, they allowed me a great deal of freedom. If they worried about my welfare, I seldom sensed it. They were never without humor or playfulness, and I always felt they would have made exceptional mothers. Fortunately for me, I had them to myself.

I would not be surprised if nowadays vacation evenings are spent watching sitcoms and, on rainy afternoons, the soaps. Do people still bring stacks of special books for vacation reading? Perhaps. But for most, I imagine, entertainment, not solitude, is the attraction. An Auntie Walton afternoon today would be an oddity and, for most people, a colossal bore. Not enough spare moments now to be filled, molded and shaped. The Pepsi generation skitters and dances raucously toward self-fulfillment, searching for some meaning. These three generous and exceptional women found meaning in poetry and music, and in the processes of mind and spirit, which, unlike the genes they were unable to pass on, were generously transmitted to all who took the time to know them. Time, once freely spent and given, is, paradoxically, the enemy we race against, in our attempts simply to gain more. It is our marathon, and in the running, we have lost the meaning.

Night Music

AUNT ANNE COULDN'T SURVIVE SUMMER WITHOUT PLAYING the piano. Music was too much in her bones. And, because she was the organist at the Moravian Church in the summer, she needed a piano for practicing her preludes at home. After much discussion over how much to spend and a long search for the right instrument, she purchased a secondhand upright of reasonable quality and tone, which was delivered and placed in a corner of the living room next to the bay window.

Every Saturday morning during the school year back home in Illinois, I went to Auntie Waltons house for piano lessons, though I would much rather have been doing something else instead. The only rewarding thing about it was that I got slices of hot homemade bread with strawberry jam when my lesson was over around noon. Aunt Anne had a lot of patience, but it often wore thin when I arrived without having even looked at my lesson for the week. I hated practicing and, therefore, tried to fake my way through every session.

"Show me how it sounds," I'd say, and then proceed to copy her technique and play the piece by ear.

"You didn't practice at all this week, did you?" she'd remark sternly.

"Yes I did, yes I did," I'd reply, lying as convincingly as possible.

"Sure doesn't sound like it to me," Aunt Mary would respond from the kitchen, "don't try to fool your Aunt Anne!"

"Even though it may not seem like it, I really did," I told them, "but I had trouble with this part right here." Surreptitiously, I'd point to a troublesome fingering or a run. "Just play it again so I can get it right this time." Then, she'd remind me that my lessons were free and ask why in the world she should waste her precious time if all I did was come to a lesson and do what I should have been doing at home during the previous week?

But my aunties knew there was real musical talent in my background and Aunt Anne was determined not to give up. The plan was to bring it out and nurture it instead. For that reason, I had little excitement about the acquisition of a piano at the cottage, fearing that a condition of my summer vacation would be the torture of playing drills and scales. To my relief, she must have decided not to overdo a good thing and promised not to make me spend more than fifteen minutes a day at the piano.

"Although it would be nice," she said firmly, "if you would play on your own once in awhile. You don't want to disappoint your old Aunt Anne."

Instead, I continued begging her to play for me and had little difficulty getting her to relent. Sometimes on rainy days, she'd play Debussy, McDowell and Bach for several hours while I turned the pages, or we'd sing together from the *Methodist Hymnal* and *The Golden Book of Song* until she was so tired she couldn't play any more.

But best of all was music after I had gone to bed. "Only if you've been a good girl," she'd tease in answer to my request, and as I lay in bed she'd begin. Those melodies enveloped rain or wind or the deep, unfathomable softness of the night with a mantle of breath-tingling, utter joy. Sometimes I could see the moon through the bedroom window. Sometimes the smell of wood smoke from the fireplace drifted in. She would sweep through Chopin, Beethoven and Grieg with the energy of a sudden hailstorm and generally end with one of my favorite Brahms waltzes. Each time she stopped, I was afraid it was the end and would shout, "Just one more. Please, play just one more?" I reveled in the weightless, blanketed comfort of bed, the chords and the resolves, and when the final reverberations folded into stillness, I longed for sleep so that no other sound could subtract from their perfection.

Aunt Anne's talent was something to be envied. I honestly wished someday to play as she did, but becoming a musician was a struggle I doubted I would ever master. Ignoring notes, playing by ear and doodling instead seemed easier, and as a consequence, I never learned to read music well. Instead, I imagined sitting at the piano and suddenly astounding everyone with a brilliant polonaise. I would play it flawlessly, magically, and make my Aunt Anne proud! Headlines would read, "Unknown pianist astounds the world with a breathtaking performance of unbelievable interpretation and skill."

Reporters would clamor for interviews and ask, "How could you suddenly play like that?"

"I don't know," I'd answer, "it just flows from within. I don't even understand it myself." There would be invitations to perform worldwide, and no one would ever even suggest that I need practice again.

Running water would be heard in the bathroom. Then Aunt Anne would quietly enter the bedroom, undress in the dark, adjust the window wider, and slip into bed.

"Good night, my child," she'd whisper. Imagined talent would yield sadly to reality. I would hear her settling into the pillow and the sound of slowed breathing. Soon we'd both slip into dreaming, Brahms' Waltz in A Flat still subliminally sweet.

Morning Catch

THERE WAS A UNIQUE SOUND TO FISHING BOATS' MOTORS; A slightly irregular, deep and sonorous "chug, chug," punctuated with occasional misfires and pops. Engine sounds could be detected far out in the lake as boats worked their way in slowly, several at a time, hulls low in the water. They were loaded down with lake trout, whitefish and chubs. At least once a week I waited with Auntie Waltons at Anderson's Dock to choose the perfect fish for dinner, breathing the commixture of fish and gasoline that never seemed to dissipate. It permeated everything. The chubby white boats reversed engines as the fishermen approached the dock, flipped their bumpers, and with time management perfected, unloaded their catch. No one could help but be a participant in that orchestration.

Wearing clumsy hip boots and protective black rubber aprons covered with scales and fish slime, they snatched the flopping fish by their gills with hooks, scaled them in seconds on large wooden platforms, and shoved them in assembly-line fashion from one worker to another. A swift flick of a sharp knife and they were gutted, hosed clean, packed in wooden crates, and covered with crushed ice for shipment. As a time saver, however, as many fish as possible were cleaned on the boat trip in. Entrails were tossed into the water, and sea gulls followed closely in noisy, swooping, querulous hordes, dipping several at a time into the water and fighting over scraps of flesh before they had a chance to sink beneath the oily wake of the boat.

Despite careful scrubbing and hosing, fish scales were scattered everywhere like glistening flakes of mica in the sun. They lingered and dried, and were reminders not only of our debt for dinner to the fish, the fishermen and the water that nurtured both, but to our sociality as well. Gulls exchanged perches on pilings the remainder of the morning and foraged for bits of forgotten morsels. For long periods, they rested placidly on the ridge pole of the barn-red, weathered building. Their signatures (accumulated droppings) competed with artistic signatures of wandering yachtsmen, who throughout the years had recorded, like genteel graffiti, names of their boats and the years they sailed them on the roof and siding of the barn.

By 11:00 A.M. the flurry of activity ended. The nets had been wound in preparation for the next trip out. Car doors slammed and fishermen left for home and coffee in their kitchens. They had begun work at 4:00 in the morning, traveling far out in the deep parts of the lake to lay new nets and pull in the old. Occasionally in early morning, if the wind was right and I was half awake, I could hear the sound of boats chugging out of the bay toward the buoys and nets, held at the surface of the water with aluminum or glass floats. Storms often washed loose floats to shore where they were collected by tourists. I draped them with string on the wall above my bed.

Aunt Mary usually handled our fish purchases. Both hands were needed to support a large fish held for her approval, as many were two feet or more in length. Acceptable in size, they were then weighed, wrapped and stowed in her wicker market basket. Occasionally, she bought whitefish livers, a sweet, exquisite, but expensive delicacy that, surprisingly, had no fishy

flavor. Lightly floured, they were sautéed in bacon fat, seasoned with a little salt, pepper, a bit of scraped onion and perfected with dribbles of fresh lemon juice. This was a favorite dish of fishermen, savored only by those who could obtain the livers while they were most fresh.

The aromas emanating from backyard smoke houses throughout the peninsula were intoxicating and magnetic after the chub run was over. Every other back yard sported a small, rough cedar building about the size of a winter fishhouse. I was agog with the sight of rack after rack of six-to-eight-inch fish hanging by their tails on nails. Oil dripped from a hundred shiny, yellowing bodies to the warm coals below. We savored them for lunch or picnic treats. After fishing season ended, however, the odor was of fresh tar from the nets spread out in fields for mending. Four or five fishermen stood with a portion of the net in one hand and shuttle in the other, skillfully repairing holes in the large black nets or the finely woven white ones, which were used for snaring chubs. That scene had been repeated for centuries by fishermen in Norway, and was duplicated by their descendants in the stony fields of Door County.

In the early 1940s, large, ugly scars were noticed on the sides of many fish. Sometimes one was hauled in with several parasitic lamprey eels attached to its side and belly, and many eels were caught singly in smaller nets. The efficiency of their rapier teeth and the configuration of their mouths was truly horrifying and repulsive. Soon catch sizes diminished, and one by one commercial fishing boats began to disappear. They languished like ancient beached fossils along shorelines, their paint peeling in the sun, their porthole's vacant eyes peering down the shore. Only a few fishermen near Death's Door remained. Although eel population has been reduced by electrifying entrances to breeding streams, commercial fishing has never returned as a viable industry. Since the Coho and Chinook salmon were introduced and trout and whitefish restocked in the lake, deep-sea sport fishing has become popular. But now, fishermen are warned to limit their intake because of mercury levels.

It had been development and progress on the Great Lakes which inadvertently undid commercial fishing and, consequently, a way of life. At that time, there were no concerns about PCBs or contaminants. Nevertheless, the raking jaws of the lamprey were just as devastating, and that devastation stemmed from the beginnings of waterway commercialization from the Welland Canal westward.

The years following The War had brought irreparable changes in our lives which we never sensed occurring. With the end of gasoline rationing and knowledge of a wider world to be experienced, a nation of vagabonds and weekend tourists shook off hometown provincialism and took to the open road. Door County responded quickly. Old boats, so picturesquely decaying on beaches, were removed as hazards and eyesores, the docks became marinas, and boathouses were upgraded to art galleries and museums as tourist attractions. Now scarce fish were diverted to markets willing to pay high prices, and whitefish livers became unavailable. The familiar aromas that marked those early years were exchanged for the odor of French fries. The fishing industry, a once-essential component of summer life on our once bountiful inland sea, was gone forever.

Waxwings and Others

NEARLY EVERY DAY SOMEONE IN THE HOUSEHOLD CONSULTED the bird book always handy on a table near the living room picture window. Bluebirds, indigo buntings, vireos, pewees, phoebes and assorted warblers frequented the yard, field and woods behind the house. Effortlessly, we were turned into avid bird watchers. Uncommon sightings or mockingbird calls from one secreted place after another in the darkening evening woods became events in which everyone was called quickly to participate.

Ornithologists frequently gave quite boring evening lectures (at least in the children's opinion) in the Village Hall. A few dedicated birders were invited to participate in day-long gull-banding expeditions on several islands way out in the lake. Picking their way amongst smooth white rocks, pebbles, gull eggs, fleeing chicks and screeching adults, they had the honor of crimping metal bands around small pink legs hour after hour until most of the birds were banded.

One summer, a bald eagle captured with an injured wing drew the curious to see the bird close up during its late afternoon feeding. Onlookers gaped with the same fascination for gore as ambulance chasers gape at victims of an accident.

Confined to a large cage for saftey's sake, ornithologists and a caring crew were determined to nurse it back to health and hoped for its eventual release. "Don't get anywhere near it," we were warned. "It could rip your finger right off. And be as quiet as possible while it's feeding. We don't want to disturb it." Then someone would sacrifice a large fish to the waiting bird. Within seconds the eagle impaled the thrashing animal with its stiletto talons, gripping the poor thing fast and furiously ripping strands and hunks of flesh from the quivering carcass with its razor-sharp beak. The entire experience left no doubt as to why the eagle was chosen as the symbol of American prowess. Nature in the raw brought shivers, and at the same time, gratitude that we human beings were not likely to be so hunted and dismembered.

But when Cedar Waxwings paused in their migration, settling in flocks on trees at the edge of the front yard, Aunt Mary laid on the grass great long strings of different thicknesses and lengths, saved from the previous year. Soon the birds flew down, several at a time, grabbing the segments of twine in their beaks and struggling to rise with it, their saucy tufts and red-and-yellow markings distinguishing their efforts like busy little corporals. As many as nine or ten of them consorted to carry off the string. Flying as high as possible, the long ends of white twine dangled across the ground until they dropped their awkward burden in the field below. Returning to settle once again, they would claim another string as if they understood and wanted to extend our pleasure. Then, in sudden, simultaneous flight, they would leave for a patch of berries or a tree, revisiting periodically for several days to entertain us before they disappeared. We rewound and saved the strands to use again the following spring.

The Oshkoshers

JULY AND AUGUST IN THE 1940S WERE MONTHS IN WHICH three proper spinsters slid easily into the netherworld of cards, dice, alcohol and slot machines, led by two female Pied Piper English teachers from Oshkosh, Wisconsin. Catherine Joslyn and Mildred Leyda rented a cabin tucked among the maples and cedars several yards south of ours, and we spent a good deal of time together over the next twenty years, frequently over poker and cocktails, vices to which my aunts had been unaccustomed.

Nevertheless, they relished every minute of such novel revelry but at the same time, were determined to maintain an aloof transcendence of it by repeating the phrase, "Enough is enough," like a mantra. After dinner and several hours of poker around the card table, ice cubes would be pebbles in the bottom of Aunt Mary's and Aunt Helen's glasses. Aunt Anne tee-totaled her way through Seven-Card-Stud, Baseball and Woolworth. The Oshkoshers on the other hand, would already be on their second beer or bourbon. With few exceptions, if the Waltons were offered a "freshener upper," they refused, mouths solidly set, implying that they were opposed to such excesses even if no one else was, and could not be compromised. Aunt Anne mouthed, "Enough is enough," most often, as if to save her sisters from the slippery slope to dissipation while she sipped her Ginger ale and arranged poker chips on her corner of the card table.

High school English teachers in Oshkosh for many years, The Girls shared a house in winter, spent vacations together, and became two of my most influential mentors. Catherine taught creative writing and read poetry, sometimes professionally, despite almost total deafness since childhood. Her voice, like many of the hearing impaired, was a little flat and singsongy, which only enhanced the poetry she recited, and we listened to her words with rapt attention. She had an analytical mind and extensive literary background, in addition to being quick-witted and sensitive. Both she and I had been adopted, although she at a later age than I. She had struggled to overcome the emotional effects of a necessary adoption by her only relative, along with the isolation imposed by deafness. In her determination to overcome adversity, she learned lip reading and put herself through college.

Mildred was a gangly six feet tall, had reddish blonde hair and a fair complexion splashed with fading freckles. She was so skilled at dramatization that I imagined she could have waltzed even a dull adverbial phrase off the pages of her classroom textbooks. During our evening gatherings, we were kept in stitches with her imitations of off-key opera singers and dowagers' serious but trite presentations at local Women's Clubs. She spoke with such hysterically funny inflections and accents that laughter plus the liquid we had ingested frequently sent us rushing to the bathroom before we lost control. Sometimes, she'd don a gaudy housecoat or nightgown, position herself in front of the fireplace and, as if on stage, present her skit to the expectant audience. How she would have loved the "Lime Jello, Marshmallow, Cottage Cheese Surprise" song sung by the classical music commedian, Anna Russell. Most hilarious was Mildred as

Carmen, gyrating wildly on the hearth, clenching a rose in her teeth. I wished I had teachers like they in my school at home! Summer seemed totally incomplete until The Girls arrived with their stacks of books, playing cards, dice, crossword puzzle books and novels, bottles of bourbon and scotch, and a winter's horde of pennies for slot machines and poker games. We all became inseparable companions, charmed by their unconventionality, lack of pretense and their delicious touch of forbidden worldliness.

From the beginning, I knew we would be the best of friends. They were unorthodox nonconformists and certainly atypical of any teachers I had known. Furthermore, they didn't treat me like a child. "We'll try not to let her be a pest," Aunt Mary assured them on first introduction, her arm cradling my shoulder.

"Oh, don't ever worry about that," they replied with a we-know-how-to-handle-it look. "We'll tell her when to go home." Then, in concealed aside to me, they countered, "You just wander over any time you feel like it. We're always happy to have company."

Nearly every day, I sneaked over to their cabin, magnetized by their openness and occasional "damns" and "hells." We dissected my aunts' eccentric traits. We discussed Edgar Allen Poe, Shelley, Wordsworth and Keats, good books to be read, and quirks of my last year's English teachers. Things I'd written over winter I saved for their honest and encouraging critique in summer, and their inspiration carried me throughout the year. Perennial teachers, as all teachers are, they'd ask, "Well, how did you feel about that?...What made you like that story?...What makes you say that?...How could you rearrange that sentence?" all questions targeting reasoning, analysis and interpretation. They listened to my grievances, tales of mistreatment and lack of understanding. They listened intently to my deepest secrets without breaking my confidence. "Give those girls a little peace," my aunts often admonished, forbidding me to visit for several days. "Maybe they'd like some time to themselves for a change!"

Fishing was another activity we had in common. I

frequently accompanied them to the old coal dock in Sister Bay with Mildred clutching their long bamboo fishing poles against the outside of the car doors. There, we hoped for good-sized bass to hit on our huge nightcrawlers. It was a real treat not to have to share these two fellow fisherwomen with anyone else and enjoy jokes told only for my benefit for a change. I cherished their assurances that I was special and was flattered with the adult relationship they offered.

They were good therapy for my mother, too, for they never stopped boosting her morale and confidence. Becoming a widow in the 1940s after thirty years of marriage, she had slid from princess to near pauper status, a single mother with no marketable work skills. Accustomed to a large house and maid, she was suddenly thrown into the world of work with only several small pieces of property, grit, determination, a few good friends and a small Social Security check as a safety net.

"Come on over, Nell," the Oshkoshers would say warmly when she arrived for a week's vacation from her job to see me. "We'll bend elbows and play Jacks or Better and a little Put and Take." I counted the poker chips and added everybody's ante. The following winters, we saved our pennies in bonbon tins, anticipating the indulgence of our base passions around the card table near the fireplace on chilly, rainy, summer evenings.

Some time in the 1940s, Wisconsin banned slot machines and, consequently, spoiled Mildred's, Catherine's and Aunt Mary's greatest pleasure. But during the years they were still legal, a decision would be made the day before to explore the other side of the peninsula the following morning, find old gravel roads leading to lighthouses and rocky beaches, and then complete the outing with lunch at the Greenwood Tavern or The Ivanhoe. Throughout the day and until after the dinner hour, the atmospheres of both places were comfortable and friendly. Not yet transformed by nighttime revelers, they were the only places to serve lunches. Dark, well-varnished wooden tables, the sweet malty aroma of fresh beer and grilled steak sandwiches, the sound of slot machines grinding out lemons, cherries and bells, and visiting with local cronies we'd not ordinarily meet, offered a spicy diversion unavailable to "respectable" women under normal circumstances. The Waltons set strict limits on their gambling, except for Aunt Mary who seemed always game for more. Aunt Anne felt she'd "fallen" if she wagered much more than three or four quarters. Mildred and Catherine however, set higher limits and won and lost coins with abandon. It was their summer, and they had saved in order to enjoy it to the fullest.

"We'll keep her in line, Nell," The Girls assured my mother before she'd leave again for home. "Don't worry about a thing. You've got the world by the tail, you know. Keep up the good job, and remember, we're all behind you." I cannot imagine what that support must have meant to her as we kissed goodbye and waved her up the hill, thankful for not having to face the long drive home ourselves. The Oshkoshers were women who were able to bridge several generations. Successful, self-confident, lovers of children, they brought fresh perspectives about the world to all our lives. Teaching and challenging without my realizing it, they raised me, too, and in turn I gave them all the love and admiration a child could muster.

Catherine hung the watercolor of Ephraim I had painted in my later teens, its hotels and steeples set against the bluff, on the wall of her room in the nursing home. When she died of Parkinson's disease years later, one of her close friends phoned me long distance to see if she could have it as a remembrance. "It was something she loved so much," she told me, "and she thought of the many good times all of you shared together every time she looked at it." Nowadays, I think of the Oshkoshers each time I read a poem, shuffle a deck of cards or cast a line into our small lake for bass. Their cottage door still opens, their voices as recognizable as returning blackbirds trilling through the air of spring. "Oh, come on," I still can hear them say. "Let's play just one more game of Put and Take and then we'll say good night!"

"Well, maybe—Just one more."

Moonlight

MOTHER WAS VISITING AND OUR SPECIAL SUMMER FRIENDS, the Oshkosh girls, Mildred and Catherine, had just arrived. We all decided to picnic together the following evening and chose Moonlight Bay as a remote spot to be all by ourselves. It was late in the afternoon when we pulled off the gravel road, parked our cars over the wild grasses and struggling beach peas, and carried our baskets and picnic paraphernalia to the shore.

Most beaches on the Lake Michigan side of the peninsula are extensive stretches of wide white dunes. This more northern area was rocky with grey-white tables of stone, ledges that descended an inch or two in height, approximately one hundred feet or so from the shore into the water of the little bay. We found a flat place to unfold our blankets and then took off our shoes. The rocks were still warm from a day of sun. Depressions of varying sizes, worn by centuries of waves and sand, retained tepid pools of water from the mornings' waves and included stranded crayfish, freshwater clams and tiny skating bugs. I stamped water from the puddles, pried open shells and annoyed crayfish by the hour. We waded, explored, collected driftwood, and examined weeds and flowers until supper time. The picnic baskets were finally opened, and we happily savored mounds of sliced ham and deviled eggs, lettuce from the garden and, at the end, cake, a convenient complement to picnics. Then we stretched out, cradled our heads in hands behind us, breathed in satisfaction, and attempted to digest it all.

The sun was setting by then on the western side of the peninsula. Our bay on the east, and all the trees around it, mellowed into gold, then into a rosy mauve that swallowed up the gilded waters and, imperceptibly, slipped everything about us into the soft half-light of dusk. Aunt Helen repacked our picnic gear, except for the blankets, then sat with the rest of us as we dabbed our toes in the warm pools and talked of going home. But the breeze and water moved gradually into a soft custard evening that restrained us unrelinquishingly. The moon appeared, at first soft yellow, then, as it rose higher, transformed to brilliant white. Constellations appeared; the dippers, belt of Orion and Cassiopia's Chair, which my aunts dubbed "The Walton W." Aunt Anne knew most about stars and pointed out the brightest of the other groupings like Andromeda and Cepheus.

Though it was getting late, and time, they said, for me to be in bed, no one moved to go. It was as if everyone felt the final aria had not yet been completed and that we should wait for it. "This is a night worth staying up for," Aunt Mary countered. "She can sleep tomorrow!" So we kept sitting. Then, without a preview, shimmering sheets of green, pink and white Northern Lights appeared against the stars, wide curling ribbons of light pulsing from north to south. They curled and swept like massive, undulating curtains of pastel gauze, orchestrated by some mesmerizing great mystery on a colossal stage.

For what seemed like hours, we marveled at the variation of their movements, the moon, the stars and voluptuous breeze that complimented and intensified sight with the other sense of touch.

"There is a poem," Catherine whispered reverently, "just

written for this night.

"'Say listen,'" she breathed softly,

"'How would ya like to take a bath,

In moonlight?'" We were immersed in it. Drowning in its splendor.

"'Can't ya just see yourself take a runnin' dive

Into a pool of glowin' blue,'" she continued, her voice fondling the words like the water that was fondling the shore,

"'And feel it glidin' all over ya,

And around ya, and into ya?

Grab a star, huh? Use it for soap.

Beat it up into bubbles and white, sparkling foam,

Roll and swash.

Gee.

I'd just like ta bet

You could wash your soul clean,

In moonlight.'"

No one spoke when she finished. The moment had been so transcendent, it defied any words of definition. An attempt would have been a sacrilege. But, there would be no forgetting. We stayed at the beach, marveling, until about 2:00 in the morning, and then, when the Aurora Borealis faded, left for home. Over the years, Catherine recited Charles A. Weaver's "Moonlight" on appropriate occasions, in reverence to that night's dazzling display. It was an experience that would continue to inspire me for the rest of my life.

Years later, during my years at Rockford College, I continued spending summers in Door County. But vacation was cut short the first year in order to comply with a college requirement in August. It was customary for freshmen to pass an oral examination in speech the week before classes began. Those who passed, and few did, were exempt. Like many my age, I had little self-confidence, and I think I had less than most because of a disability in math. I felt dumb in general and was so terrified speaking before groups that my voice quivered, and I feared my mind would blank out completely. On one occasion

in junior high school, I'd forgotten everything I'd planned to say and was asked to sit down, never to give my report at all. So, for a week or more before the oral exam I worried and fretted. From what I'd been told by everyone, the extemporaneous exam was difficult and the professor tough on everybody. "So what kinds of things does she ask you to talk about?" I asked some of the other girls.

"Who knows?" I was told. "It's likely to be anything. All I know is, I didn't pass, and neither did anybody else I know."

"What would be the most far-out thing she could ask me?" I wondered to myself, and "what would be the hardest thing to talk about? It could even be something like, 'What did you do this summer?'" I conjectured haphazardly, and just in case, planned word-for-word what I would say. If she asked me to expound on something else, I'd just tell her that what I really wanted to talk about was what I did this summer. She just might respond with, "All right, go ahead then." At least it would be worth a try.

The dreaded day arrived. I was admitted to an empty room with a professor dressed in a bright blue suit (today it might be called a "power suit"), her white hair brushed sternly to the back of her head. Large gold earrings with onyx centers emphasized her intimidating figure. "Well, Miss Bliss," she said curtly, "most students think this is going to be easy, but I'll guarantee it is not. You have to be pretty good to get out of my class! It is important that you know how to face an audience and that you develop perfect elocution, and that's what my class will teach you. Now, I want you to stand up there, in front. That's it. And I'll sit back here."

I stood facing her, quaking and ashen-faced, in front of the blackboard in that empty room and doubted if I would ever make it through college, let alone that harrowing moment.

"There. That's fine," she said, seating herself in one of the classroom desks and looking at me intently. "Now Miss Bliss, you have about five minutes. Tell me. How did you spend your summer?"

I gave my rehearsed speech flawlessly. No "ahs" or "ums." I began to describe the place I loved, the imagery of it and the people I knew so intimately. It tumbled out in a perfect order that culminated with, not only facts, but recollections of the influences those experiences had had on a developing personality. "There is a poem," I concluded, "which is a summation of the magic Door County has given me throughout the many summers I have spent there." Suddenly, I was the embodiment of Catherine as she recited her poem that special evening. "'Say listen!'" I questioned the professor softly, "'How would ya like to take a bath, in moonlight…?'"

When I finished, she was silent. Finally, "Beautiful!" She shook her head in disbelief. "Beautiful!" she said again. "I think you ought to know you're one of the very few who have ever done so well. Certainly, there's a lot you could learn from taking my class, but under the circumstances—well, I just couldn't require it."

It must have been about seventeen years later when my own children were eight and ten that we placed the lawn chairs in the back yard and traced the moon's rise through and then above the branches of the black walnut tree to the east.

At first, it appeared soft yellow, then was transformed to brilliant white. The sweet scent from Nicotiana which grew so densely in the garden enveloped us with every breath, and our bare feet delighted in the cool, damp comfort of the grass. We found the Big and Little Dippers and "The Walton W," and searched for more.

It was one of those warm, soft custard evenings, and it held us unrelinquishingly. "There is a poem," I told the children, "written, I think, just for this moment. "'Say listen,'" I quoted softly, "'How would ya like to take a bath,

In moonlight?'"

Summer Hunt

WE LIMITED DRIVING DURING THE WAR, PLANNING OUR excursions carefully. On Friday or Saturday evenings around 5:30, we ate our supper early, satisfied our need for doing something different and the aging Chrysler's thirst for gasoline, and set out to hunt for deer. When visitors stayed with us, they could be assured that on weekends they would be treated to an hour or more of, "Oh stop! Stop! Over there. See it?"

"Where? Where? I don't see it at—"

"All right. Now I do. Right at the back of the meadow. Look. See? There's five of them. No, there's another. Six!" The car's interior space would be crisscrossed with arms and fingers pointing in all directions, and one of my aunts usually complained about the rudeness of putting fingers in front of other people's faces. Someone in the car kept tally and each year we assessed the deer population of Peninsula State Park by comparison counting. Deer hunting became a Walton ritual that endured for at least twenty years—a ritual requiring no license, no park fee or sticker. They never grew tired of the pursuit, though I have no doubt guests sometimes did. Perhaps in the act of looking so intently for antlers and white tails they found pleasure in not having anything about which to disagree.

Aunt Helen drove through the park with exasperating slowness. She knew exactly in which meadows deer were most likely to be spotted, and each week she chose one of two main routes to get to them. Sometimes it was the high road and sometimes the low road, and we often sang, "You take the high road and I'll take the low road," as we drove. Along the way, we stopped at all the lookouts, getting out of the car to watch the sunset and silhouetted pines that jutted into the evening light. Each lookout presented a different panorama, and by the time we reached the next one, we viewed a new presentation of water, cloud and color, a new spectacle of setting sun and sky.

Aunt Helen announced road names like a scenic bus driver. "There are the Twelve Apostles," she would inform us as we approached the familiar stand of old pines, an island in the middle of the road. During one winter, however, a tree had been felled by the Wisconsin State Forest Service, and we were saddened the following summer to find that only eleven pines remained. It was Judas who was missing, we supposed, and thereafter, the grouping seemed to have lost its dramatic effect.

In July, I took my caterpillar box with me in the car. When we drove by fields of milkweed, it was agreed that we would stop so I could look for Monarch butterfly worms, and my box soon became filled with them. Their sheer numbers made Aunt Mary shiver, especially if any escaped or I allowed them to crawl along my arm.

Driving through state park campgrounds was avoided. The aunties thought of campers as interlopers, disfiguring the landscape with their sagging clothes lines, soggy bathing suits and gritty, gray bath towels. "They're litter spreaders," Aunt Mary complained. "You tell me how in the world they can ever keep themselves clean!" In addition, they were usurpers of space that was more appropriate for the 'coons and foxes, which we also saw during our weekly reconnoitering. (How could we have missed them? We spent so many hours there.)

There were times when Aunt Helen parked the car and turned off the motor near a particular meadow known to be frequented by deer. "They won't appear," she said, "if they hear a motor running. Besides, it saves gasoline and helps cool off the engine." We'd wait, with no one allowed to speak except in whispers, for fear of scaring off the deer. Those were the times I understood the expression, "he almost jumped out of his skin." I thought I would die from sitting so still. "Let's go," I'd beg, ready to explode with childish boredom. "Maybe they're down another road." Nevertheless, we would continue to sit, for what seemed like hours, until Aunt Helen made up her own mind to start the engine again. As dusk fell over the woods, the ritual ended at last, and as a special treat if there was no dessert at home, I was sometimes able to convince them to stop at the

ice cream parlor for cones or hot fudge sundaes. "A perfect end to a perfect day," they'd say, as they licked the dribbles of chocolate from the edge of their cones in order to keep their napkins from becoming soggy with the melting goo. Those comments were as ritualistic as the weekly hunt. In the meantime, I amused myself by observing how differently each one approached the business of eating cones. Aunt Anne always pushed the cream down into the cup with her tongue, eventually causing it to drip through its bottom. "You eat yours the way you like and I'll do the same with mine," she'd snap defensively when criticized for potential sticky dribbles on her dress or the car seat. Aunt Helen dispatched hers by orderly nibbling around the edge, while Aunt Mary simply ate hers without any ostentation whatsoever, much as I did.

As the years progressed, others joined in the deer hunts, and I always surmised the hunts were my aunts's original idea, though I have no way to prove it. What I do know is that the number of deer counted by summer residents on evening forays during The War years was often a topic of conversation and became a summer community pastime. For me, as well as the guests at our house, it was a passive activity in which all ages could participate on an equal footing. Together in the car, it was a time of shared conversation and closeness. It was a time of bonding with each other over sunsets, and of all things, even over the white flags of bounding deer.

Community Sing

"WE'RE HERE TO SING, NOT JUST TO MOVE OUR LIPS!" THIS WAS Mrs. Byfield's frequent admonition in July at the beginning of each Ephraim Community Sing held in the auditorium of the Village Hall. Letting her body and lips go limp, she would imitate an apathetic singer. "Not uhs," she would say, "but good round O-O-O's. Let's practice. Everyone say it with me now. O-O-O." In encouragement, her thumb and third digit would come together as she raised her arm above her head. Come on, move those lips. Enunciate. You know, if you're not willing to sing, you shouldn't be here!" she'd continue. "Now I'm going to be watching, so if you don't want to be embarrassed, SING."

Mrs. Byfield was a short but commanding woman who taught voice in Chicago and shared her vocal and directing expertise on summer Sunday evenings at the Village Hall from 7:00 to 9:00. She was able to incite such enthusiasm in her audience that the sing became a must for almost every tourist and villager and an institution with undiminishing appeal for many years. Despite her diminutive size, her ebullient self-confidence contributed to an imposing presence, and well-fitting couture suits and dresses augmented her air of authority. Heavy bracelets dangled from her wrists. Her nails were meticulously polished and her fingers adorned with large, artistic silver rings and diamonds. She was the first person I'd met who wore several rings on each hand, including on the index fingers.

Aunt Anne, in a simple, well-starched, homemade cotton dress, would seat herself at the upright piano as people filed into the small auditorium and *The Golden Book of Song* and *Moravian Hymnal* was passed to everyone. By the end of the vacation season, there was sometimes a capacity crowd and more chairs had to be placed along the back wall of the room. Mrs. Byfield explained, as she did each weekend for newcomers, that the first half of the sing would be from *The Golden Book of Song*, the second half from the hymnal.

"Everyone will have a chance to choose your favorite," she assured us. "Just raise your hand and shout out the number of your tune when I call on you. But don't be surprised when I select one or two myself. That's a director's privilege. Also," she would continue, "it's our custom to conclude our evening with, 'Eternal Father, Strong to Save,'" known at the time as, the Navy hymn.

"Oh hear us when we cry to thee for those in peril on the sea," was a prayer we all sang from the depths of our beings, and firsthand knowledge of the often treacherous lake just a few feet from the door of the hall, made that hymn all the more relevant. But, when The War finally ended, "Now The Day Is Over" replaced it.

"Certainly, that is a fitting and lovely hymn for such a beautiful evening," Mrs. Byfield would remind us. "And how privileged we all are to be able to share the joy of music and song in such a wonderfully special place." Aunt Anne took this as her cue and shifted her bottom on the piano bench, adjusted her gold-rimmed bifocals, and made certain she had the correct pedal beneath her large brown and white spectator shoes. "Who will begin?" Mrs. Byfield would question. Several would raise their hands.

"Number 106, 'The Old Oaken Bucket,'" someone would shout, and Aunt Anne would begin a short prelude, playing the first and last line as Mrs. Byfield raised her arms before moving her baton as a signal to begin. We went through them all: "Loch Lomond," "Old Black Joe" "The Farmer in the Dell," "Santa Lucia," "In the Gloaming," "Dixie," "When Johnny Comes Marching Home," "Drink to Me Only With Thine Eyes," each sung as close to the pleasure of our instructor as possible, who directed us as if she were drilling the King's College Choir.

"No, no, no! Stop!" she would sometimes interject, as our voices trailed into a surprised silence. "You all sound as if you're PLODDING through the rye! This is a happy young man. He's going to meet his lover, not attend her funeral!" Then she'd sing unenthusiastically, dragging her voice in playful imitation, while we giggled at her and at ourselves. "This is a happy tune. See? It says 'lively' right up in the left-hand corner of the page. Now. Let's start over and put some life into it."

Most fun to sing was, "My Name is Solomon Levi" and "The Young Minstrel Boy," which, after we had sung each independently, was combined as a round, one half of the room singing one tune while the second half sang the other. It took precise counting and concentration to make it all end up correctly. This and other rounds were often Mrs. Byfield's choice, as were "Sweet and Low," "All Through the Night," "The Last Rose of Summer," and other more subdued songs which she picked as a way of preparing us psychologically for the hymn singing which was to follow.

Sitting between Aunt Helen and Aunt Mary, I waited anxiously for the hymn singing to begin. Aunt Mary said "I Walk Through the Garden Alone," "What a Friend We Have in Jesus," and "The Old Rugged Cross" were three of her least favorites. "It's trashy music," she stated emphatically, seriously hoping no one would request any of them. I did at least twice during each summer and took unbelievable pleasure in her groans, grimaces, and protestations.

Now Aunt Anne had assumed the more pious look of a hymn player, wearing the "Gawd" look on her face despite her battle with the old piano. She always pronounced it, "Gawd," rather than, God, which embarrassed us all, because it seemed so pretentious. By this time, our voices were warmed up. We had become comrades in song and spirit, and the hymns were symbolic of our togetherness. We sang as a great choir: Bach, Haydn, Beethoven, the magnificent songs of the fourteenth century, and the social activist hymns of the eighteen hundreds. From those hymns, I acquired a host of new vocabulary words—assuage, ascribe, fervent, clime—at the same time wondering how come angels needed prostrates and, what it was that made them fall? We sang the Navy hymn, "for those in peril on the sea," with tears in our eyes, knowing that "our boys" were in mortal danger, on and under the Pacific Ocean, and were inwardly comforted by the depth and perfection of our voices.

From disparate places, young or old, we were tied to each other in song and melded into a single body. "Now the Day is Over." Our reverent voices modulated on verse five, and we left as we had been instructed, without a word, into the starry night.

We picked our way up the stone steps set into the lower bluff, a shortcut to the upper road, and laboriously wound ourselves up the Big Hill in the darkness with our flashlights and the moon. Zig-zagging from one side of the road to the other on our way to the top, we eased the steepness of the climb. Aunt Anne swung the drawstring purse dangling from her wrist back and forth as she did each Sunday, and walked pigeon-toed in a recommended exercise to strengthen the arches of her size thirteen-plus feet. Going down the hill before the sing we'd teased her by singing "Clementine," whose shoes were "herring boxes without topses," with a size of "number nine."

But on the walk home, we had been transformed. The words and music had pumiced the hard edges of our minds and tongues. At the crest of the hill, we stopped to catch our breath and gaze over the waters in the bay, saw lights blinking on the far horizon, and the church steeple silhouetted against it all, framed in the thick flood of moonlight. We were still awash in the sounds of our music. It seemed the entire universe had to have heard our singing, and that somewhere in the atmosphere our praise must be drifting, immutable, unfading, note for note. They were words and melodies awaiting capture by some unknown intelligence centuries beyond that moment in our time. Would humanity be judged by the splendor of their sounds?

The perfection of melody can be a religious experience that one aches to share and to repeat. Songs sung yesterday are the same notes as tomorrow's but played on different strings. Though a child, I knew that those luminous moments had been freely given and marked each of our lives forever. During the dark evening winters in my bed at home, I relived the breathless exhilaration of those nights at the top of the Big Hill, sang in my head, and dreamed, as I still do, of Mrs. Byfield, her baton in hand, and of Aunt Anne and "Gawd," playing the piano.

Boxes

MR. WILSON, OWNER OF THE ICE CREAM PARLOR, GAVE ME empty boxes. Nearly every day, I peered through the glass display case to count the dwindling cigars, hoping to be the first with my request. Elaborately embossed in red, green, and gold paper picturing white owls and stylized veiled women draped voluminously in brilliant cloth, they evoked images of exotic places and a curiosity over the mystique surrounding males and stogies. Cigars from the cedar boxes with tiny, well-made dove-tailed corners and miniature brass hinges and closures didn't empty so rapidly as the others. Those cigars were more expensive, and unfortunately, ladies who found those containers most durable for storing sewing notions got first choice over the requests of children. I found the thick cardboard ones just as useful anyway. One didn't have to bother with latches to open the lids, and they could easily be labeled, decorated, or stacked. Furthermore, it seemed sacrilegious to deface such delicately made things. I pictured Cubans in Havana carpenter shops, working to laboriously craft every one by hand.

Summer wintered over well in boxes, like pantry shelves stored with canned peaches, pears, and jam. My boxes held dead beetles, inch-long shiny Coleopteras with large eye-like circles on their wings, iridescent green and blue beetles of all shapes and sizes, dung beetles, and those with jagged frontal pinchers half again as long as the thorax of the bug itself. I had boxes filled with dead butterflies, giant dragonflies, red and blue "darning needles," and assorted samples of sailing knots, spliced rope, goldenrod galls, and lichens.

There were boxes of valuable "prehistoric" animal bones. Some had probably inhabited the bluff caves long before the village settled against the balsamed cliffs. Most likely, I surmised, the creatures had been shot by Indians. I looked for arrowheads but never found any. There were assorted jaw bones with wobbly fangs, hidden in the crevices we explored on the northeast bluff, horse teeth from Strege's pasture, and shin bones, porous with age and green with moss like the north side of old trees. What I accumulated was evidence of primal struggles in a place where history had not been thoroughly recorded. I was the budding archeologist fingering mysteries embodied in those bones, which, like Egyptian finds, connect all mankind in the same common dirt.

In August, my boxes housed a dozen or more white-, yellow-, and black-striped caterpillars, grazing noisily on milkweed leaves. With several feedings of fresh leaves each day, they grew large and translucent within a week and migrated to the window screen cover of their cage to rest and weave a tiny web. Then, locking their black crochet hook appendage into the spot of silk, they hung for several days like letter J's, suspended only by a small black piton. If I were lucky, I saw them begin the wild, wiggling gyrations that signaled their transformation into pale green living pendants flecked with the fool's gold of an alchemist.

Even in December, when the previous summer was history and the new one all-too-far away, that box retained the distinct aroma of the Monarchs' metamorphosis. These smells were sufficient to carry me into imaginary fields of milkweed where I collected the grey-green stalks and accompanying worms during what remained of winter, and tended them once more to butterflies. Only the crisp, transparent discards, vestiges of transmutation, remained on the stained white paper floor of their cell. But with an ear to the box, like the waves heard in old sea shells, I could hear them munching. Such retrospections were woven into my winter writing assignments and, as opposed to multiple choice questions and sentence punctuation exercises, they seemed of much greater importance. The contents of my boxes were symbolic of beginnings, endings, and renewals, discovered beyond the asphalt roads where the dusty gravel began and where the natural world pulsed with expectation, life, and uncommon discovery. Much can be stored in boxes.

A Secret Place

THE FIRST GRAVEL ROAD AT THE TOP OF THE BIG HILL HAD a split-rail fence on either side. From there, the Moravian Church could be seen, the bay and bluff beyond framing its steeple. On the right and several yards farther down the road was the Moravian cemetery, shaded by large old maples, surrounded by a wrought-iron fence, and edged with common orange day lilies. Almost opposite the cemetery, an unobtrusive path led into the woods, and unless one knew what to look for, it could easily have been missed. Only by surveying carefully for bent branches and disturbed weeds would one find the narrow trail that disappeared quickly into the brush.

I discovered my secret place during an afternoon's exploring. It seemed close enough to home to be reached quickly and still far enough away to be all mine, I decided. Once inside, the sunlight filtering into the woods at different periods of the day changed the shadows and the mood of the little area much like Monet's seasonal paintings of haystacks, and I frequently leaned against the trunk of one especially large pine and ate my lunch there. I also brought along *One Hundred and One Famous Poems* for inspiration, (William Cullen Bryant's

"Thanatopsis" being one of my favorites) and a personal writing tablet for recording deep thoughts and questions concerning life and death. Young girls make poor and melancholy poets.

"My Place" was within a stand of tall white pines that formed an enclosure from the rest of the woods and provided the comforting snugness of a house. Underfoot, the ground was dense with years of accumulated dried aromatic needles that made a comfortable cushion upon which to sit or lie down. The large shaggy tree trunks made perfect back rests as well as highways for busy, sap-collecting black ants. Lying on my back and looking up twenty-five or more feet, the straight trunks appeared to narrow and converge near their tops like the far end of a giant tunnel. Feathery needles at their tips meshed together against the sky, allowing snatches of sunlight to filter to the ground below, shifting in concert with the breeze above. To me, this was my Romantic sylvan glen, the sort of spot the poet Shelley would have appreciated; so perfect, it might be a foretaste of Heaven, I thought. If so, I should be satisfied with it. This was a near holy place which seemed inhabited by some beneficent living spirit, and I spent a great deal of time there trying to connect with it. Through the poets in my book, the beauty of my glen, and God perhaps, I hoped to be endowed with a great poetic nature, burst into the literary world, and become as famous as Wordsworth or Keats.

If I lay on my back and stared hard and long, and if the air were still, I was sure I could see pollen particles swimming in the rays of upper light, just as one sees dust in sunlight angling through winter living rooms. I wept at the beauty of it all, felt the tears slowly marking my cheek and thoroughly enjoyed myself.

But after two months or more of visiting my place, I became a little weary with it all. I had produced no great poetry, nor had I written anything in my notebook that seemed especially earth-shaking or unique. I enticed friends singly to share in my secret but was disappointed in their lack of enthusiasm for it. To them, it was simply a place in the woods. They weren't interested in spending time there and couldn't understand why I would. So, not wanting anyone to think I'd abandoned the idea of literary fame, I continued with my self-indulgent reveries alone in the woods and regretted I had attempted sharing it with anyone at all.

Late one afternoon I caught the sound of someone whistling, and instinctively moved as far away from the nearby path as possible without making any sound. Through the low, dead pine branches I could see a man moving along the path, lunch pail in hand. He was dressed in blue jeans, an old work shirt, and visored cap and was briskly navigating the shortcut to the road. I crouched behind a tree until he passed, then quickly gathered up my things and hurried home.

"You want me to show you my secret place?" I asked mother when she came to spend a few days to see how I was getting on. Consequently, one late afternoon, we parted the weeds and branches at the edge of the road and followed the path to the pines. I showed her where I'd carved my initials into a tree with my pocket knife and the deeply scarred finger where the blade had slashed it as it doubled back. I told her about writing and reading poetry there. We sat together on the soft needles and looked upward, mesmerized by the green vault of branches above. Suddenly, my secret place seemed ordinary, and for some reason I didn't understand, I felt inwardly relieved. Not only had I outgrown my secret place, I intuitively no longer felt safe there. Sharing had provided the reason to be released from it.

"Yes, it is lovely, Dear," my mother nodded when I asked her what she thought of it. "But you know, I just don't like your being here alone. It's all right, I suppose, if you're here with friends, but please, just be a little careful?"

"Oh Mom, don't worry!" I replied. "I'm PERFECTLY safe. Nobody knows I'm even around!"

Nevertheless, with mother's warning and my apprehensions there seemed little possibility of recapturing the same joy in

the spot I'd had before. I returned once or twice and mused for a few moments as if I were visiting the cemetery. The following spring, bulldozers cleared a driveway through my path, and the sound of hammering could be heard among the pines in the woods. My trees were gone, and with them, the secret place.

Some secret places are filled with painful memories and end up being buried deep within. Others have been actual locations where, in a single inspirational flash, one has found purpose and direction, or briefly grasped some understanding of God or of the universe and how his or her little life fits within it. The latter was true in my case, and I felt betrayed when the trees were removed for something so mundane as development even though the change was inevitable.

Fortunately, what we have experienced in our secret places, once identifiable in childhood in terms of trees and paths, in time merge with the broader landscape of the mind, coloring the beliefs and thoughts that define who we are. They become spiritual works of art stored in our mental gallery. Often reviewed, reconstructed, and reframed, they are displayed for a lifetime in the rooms of our minds. Each generation has need of secret places.

Waiting for the Mail

THE SOUND OF BERT THORP SHIFTING BOXES AROUND IN THE mail room could be heard from behind the wall and the closed clerk's window. What followed was a rapid, familiar, and repetitive, slip, slip, slip, as letters were dealt to the counter like cards, and the dull "thunk" of envelopes butting the end of wooden mail slots. Everyone waiting listened carefully. Judging from those sounds, one would have thought that the sorting was nearly completed and that the service window would soon be open. However, that assumption often proved false, and after ten minutes or so of additional waiting, there was the realization that no one could even begin to guess just when Bert would open the post office. Men fresh from boardrooms and schedules were eager to get to the golf course or their sailboat and were not happy wasting their precious, brief vacation time chitchatting in lines. Mutterings such as, "Gad, he's slow this morning! I'm not gonna' stand here much longer." were not uncommon, and though Bert couldn't prove who had muttered the complaint, he got the gist of what was said.

"Truck was late. I'm going as fast as I can. Darned truck is always late lately," he'd pronounce defensively from the other side of the partition. Long silences would ensue, then a little shuffling and more pauses. One wondered if those silences were purposeful on Bert's part. Maybe things would have moved faster if some people had just kept their mouths shut.

Waiting for the mail was actually a delightful event, for the post office and Village Hall drew us together like warm winter kitchens draw friends away from living rooms. It was our comfortable center like the hollow of a chilly bed and symbolic of our winter yearnings in the abstract cities where we lived apart most months of the year. In spring, like birds singing on familiar branches to reclaim old territories, and with every crevice of our cars stuffed with late decisions, we stopped at the post office before seeing to anything else in order to legitimize our summer residency.

There, we would renew last year's friendships as we waited in line for mail from the places we were attempting to forget. Though mail was anticipated, as much for the social activity involved in collecting it as for the news it brought, a letter could be an unwelcome reminder of the temporality of all Shangri Las. For those who were unfortunate enough to be called home because of an emergency or who missed the summer altogether, as I did the year a polio epidemic kept so many children quarantined, the loss was heartbreaking.

The Village Hall and post office, a single multipurpose building, was built from peninsula stone and was unlike most other local structures made of wood and painted white. It was the most impressive and substantial building in the village. The heavy wooden detailing, outlining its style in Scandinavian blue against blue sky, could easily have boasted gargoyles on its upturned eves without seeming out of place. Besides hosting the weekly community sing, the hall was a setting for rummage sales, church bazaars, art fairs, and Saturday evening movies. The movies were mostly ancient reruns. But near the end of The War, when everyone needed a hefty psychological boost and a bit of pain-assuaging fantasy, the village fathers went to a lot of trouble and expense to bring in a nationally advertised musical film intended to be shown only in large city theaters. It was questionable up until the last minute as to whether the distributor was going to let Bert have it. The reel had been contracted and already paid for by metropolitan theaters in and outside the state, and the delivery schedule was inflexible. Interrupting that chain and letting it go on good faith to our Village Hall was risky business. Our audience was picayune and certainly no competitor in the big movie circuit! The film was shown, but as I recall, someone had to drive it to Sturgeon Bay the next morning to make certain it was returned on time. Despite that well-attended extravaganza, it was Barbara Stanwick's second-rate movie, "Jeopardy," that I enjoyed best of all.

Weekday mornings between 9:00 and 11:00, people stood before the small rectangular window to collect the letters that linked them to Chicago, Indianapolis, and the points between and beyond. Our social and financial diversity was a fact we were well aware of as we waited together. But the landscape we shared was too perfect to be betrayed by irreverent, class conscious, September pretenses. Ordinarily, we would never have met and mingled. Here however, we shared everything from recipes to secrets of our winter lives. University professors, opera singers, corporate heads, fishermen, cherry pickers, and resort owners, all bided their time in line together. Freed from style by summer, the small waiting area filled with those who craved the comfort of last year's ragged sneakers, worn straw hats, casual print dresses, and old denims rolled mid-calf. On equal footing, we shared utopia together for several months, embracing and simultaneously ignoring our differences in a mystical, collective summer celebration of which I was fortunate to be a part.

"Are the boysenberries ripe yet?" Was I going to pick cherries again? Others would join the conversation, discussing the expected size of the cherry crop and speculating on how much the growers might pay per pail. The topic of cherries and berries was something I could talk about with pride. I'd been in the orchards and picked them.

"Hi there, Mr. Butler! How are ya? I forgot. Did you tell me your son had graduated from Annapolis yet or not?"

Mr. Butler taught school in winter and managed Thorp's dock in the summer. He wore whites and a white captain's cap at work and sometimes a brass-buttoned navy coat when the arrival of large launches were expected. I thought he was spectacularly handsome, visited him whenever I fished at his dock, and often rented his rowboats.

"He graduates next year," he answered.

"Say," I said with an air of importance because of what I was going to say, "I always forget to ask ya this. When your son was a plebe, did the other guys ever ask him how long he'd been in the Navy, and then he'd have to answer 'em with a poem?"

"Not that I know of. What do you mean, a poem? What poem?"

"Well, I read this book about Annapolis. And it said that every plebe had to be ready to salute and answer the question, 'How long have you been in the Navy?' by repeating:

"'*All me life, Sir.*
Me Mother was a mermaid and me father was King Neptune.
I was born on the crest of a wave and rocked in the cradle of the deep.
Seaweed and barnacles are me clothes.
The hair on me head is hemp.
Every tooth in me head is a marlin's spike, and every bone in me body is a spar.
And when I spits, I spits tar.
I'm hard, I is, I am, I are!'"

"Well, it was something like that anyhow. Didn't he ever tell you he had to say that?"

"No, I don't believe he ever said he did. That's a new one on me!"

"Gosh. Then why would they have said that in the book I wonder."

"Well, maybe they used to do that but just don't do it anymore. Maybe it is an old book," he answered, as I stood there feeling foolish, having quoted the whole poem to impress him and then discovering he knew nothing about it.

"Saw you fishing yesterday," he continued. "What did you get?"

"Oh, just little ones. I'm not buying your hellgrammites anymore though. They cost too much. Besides, yesterday I caught all mine on worms. You need more worms to sell? I've got extra. Grow 'em in a box with coffee grounds."

"Right now I've got plenty. But, if I need some, I'll be sure to let you know," he answered, patting me on the shoulder.

"Remind your aunts about the Ladies Aide meeting on Wednesday, and tell Mary not to forget the recipe she promised to bring me," remarked my aunts' friend, Verna with her usual warm smile.

Tidbits I'd picked up from conversations at home made good conversational openers. "I hear your daughter is coming tomorrow." "My aunts told me Mr. Bell is sick. I hope he's getting better." "You should drop over and see Aunt Anne's Iceland poppies. They're all in bloom now." "Weren't the northern lights last night really something? I stayed up real late watching 'em." My trivia was accepted graciously, and I felt as adult as anyone in line.

At last, the window opened, and for Bert it was business as usual. Along with dispensing mail, he could tell everyone where the accident was when the siren went off and whether the victims had to be taken to the hospital or to Dr. Sneeberger's office at 3:00 A.M. to be patched up. Did 'so-and-so' have her baby yet? Ask Bert. Who had bought the cottage at the end of Germantown Road? Just ask Bert. The post office was like a local newspaper.

"You heard about what happened at Shorewood?"

"Uh-uh."

"Well, from what I heard, two of their waitresses spent last night on Eagle Island with some boys in their launch! The boat's engine wouldn't start, and of course, they couldn't get back in time to serve breakfast. Somebody finally found out where they were when the other waitresses were questioned about it, and then a boat had to go wa-a-ay out there and pick them up in this weather! Can you believe it? Poor Mrs. Olson was beside herself with worry."

"Imagine help behaving like that. Well, I'd never give 'em a chance to pull a trick like that on me again, believe you me. I'd send 'em home in a hurry!"

Lacking phones and adequate supplies of gasoline, the best way to contact a friend, extend a dinner invitation, or arrange a get-together was to sit on one of the wide stone ledges on either side of the Village Hall steps and wait. Practically everybody showed up sometime between 10:00 A.M. and noon.

Becoming old enough to be trusted to deliver invitations or collect mail was an unwritten benchmark toward adulthood. Not only could one discover secrets of the summer neighborhood, one could assume the role of local storyteller, as well. From Bert, who knew as much about you as you did yourself since he handled your mail summer after summer, and from all who stood in line, one brought home insignificant but frequently, very interesting bits of information. Bringing news home to family or friends rather than hearing it secondhand, was something to be treasured. Often, if it were interesting enough, it could be refined and retold for several days or even weeks.

The post office was a center for social bonding and provided a sense of place and belonging. There were no field trips on faceless yellow buses contrived to fill the hours of childhood. That would have fractured the comfortable framework and familiar connections that gave summer meaning. What transpired within the village boundaries was sufficiently engrossing.

If there are centers now, blue against blue sky for childhood's definitions, they are difficult to find. Today, there are separate places for the young, the old, for those who paint, and those who exercise. The collective feeling of "us" in society seems to have dwindled. Our ancestors centered themselves around their fires, telling tales and comforting each other in the darkness. More recent counterparts may have been old small town post offices and village halls which presently are empty, white architectural museums—vestiges of lost Americana, preserved along our country roadsides. Life has gone out of them. Many have been torn down and landscaped over. Progress has buried them like old bones; except perhaps, in places where mail is not delivered and people like Bert open small windows somewhere between 9:00 and 11:00 on weekday mornings.

Spies Below the Wall

SHE WAS SO COMPLETELY UNAWARE OF US, WE COULD HAVE been a million miles away. Instead, we were only across the street, fifty or so feet away from her. As the road eased down the hill to the lakeshore, it passed in front of the house and garden where it shortly joined the lower road, the main highway through the village. A hidden, crumbling, freemasonry retaining wall bordered the edge of the upper road. Full of nooks and crannies, it was perfect for a ten-year-old to hide cigarette packages one didn't dare bring into the house. The wall and accompanying thick stand of cedar trees between it and the road below provided perfect cover for spying, and what an absolute delight it was to sit there for an hour or so, visiting, sharing stale cigarettes, and blowing smoke in Aunt Anne's direction.

She was too engrossed in delphiniums, poppies, and dividing and shaking the dirt from her day lilies to see us. If she had, I might have been sent home. But, each time she turned in our direction we quickly ducked our heads below the wall and instead, blew the smoke defiantly in the opposite direction.

"There. See? She's posing again just like she always does.

It's like she wants people to see how hard she works. Like she's wishing somebody would take her picture."

Aunt Anne removed her gold-rimmed glasses and wiped the perspiration from her brow with the back of a gloved hand and rested for a moment. A large foot in navy tennis shoes and white anklets rested on the top of the spade. I could almost see the freckles splattering the white legs that were exposed below her rolled up slacks. From my vantage point, I dissected and reassembled her primness. I dwelt unpityingly upon her small, irritating mannerisms, just as my aunts frequently did, and found power in it. The way she raised her eyebrows, the way she held her hands. The way she phrased things and pronounced her words.

"How could she miss us?" I exclaimed to my friend Evie, my voice dripping with derision. "How dumb can you get? Well, at least she can't make me carry pails of rocks from here or tell me to refold that stupid dusting paper for the umpteenth time to wipe down the stairs!"

"Did she ever have a boyfriend?" Evie asked.

"I don't know; I s'pose so," I answered. "But, I don't think she ever had a REAL one. Aunt Mary and Aunt Helen tease her about it. They said the only time she really had a date, she flubbed it. She was going to go boating with some guy and when she tried to put her foot into the boat, it moved away from the dock and she went kerplop into the water. Can't you just picture it? Must have been a riot! They said she was never very graceful. Her father sent her to music school in Chicago, so she didn't have a chance to meet too many boys."

I imagined her kissing somebody. Did she miss not having a man? Did she ever do it? How different would she be if she had had a husband? I pictured her standing in the garden with her children.

"Did you ever think that maybe she could be your real mother?" Evie suggested. "She used to have red hair you know. Maybe that's the reason they take you for the summer. Maybe it's a secret nobody knows."

"Yeah, I thought about it once," I answered. "That would be somethin' wouldn't it! But somehow, I don't think so. I think I'd be able to tell."

I began to feel a little sorry for Aunt Anne but didn't want to show it. That would spoil the fun of being behind the wall, which was as exciting as lying on the bed in Mayna's upstairs bedroom, (another summer friend) blowing smoke through the screen, and listening for her grandma NaNa to leave the summer kitchen and start up the stairs. For a week or so, until it rained and soaked our cigarettes, that spot behind the wall was a wonderfully clandestine place for defiance and releasing nastiness. Beyond enjoying rebelliousness however, I did feel

sorry for Aunt Anne and a little guilty about exposing her faults to somebody who shouldn't know about them. I knew she "loved me to pieces," as she so often said, and I knew how betrayed she would have felt if she had known all the unfair things I said about her. Picked on by her sisters for the way she held her hand, or posed, or drank her juice, I was the one who most always consoled her, and now I was doing the same thing as everyone else. "You don't love me at all," I remember her complaining tearfully to her sisters. I was certainly a mean-spirited conspirator along with them. But, heady with my importance and safe behind the wall, I continued heaping judgments on her.

"They're really awfully good to you though," Evie protested, who seldom criticized her parents no matter how angry they made her.

"Well, you just don't know what my aunts are like," I retorted, wanting to have something to complain about and a reason to continue my sham. "You should live with them!"

We moved from the wall and secreted the package again between the stones. That evening after dinner, I walked to the ice cream parlor and bought ice cream for everybody as a treat. Aunt Anne peeled the peaches, sliced them and arranged them on the top.

"My girl!" she said, as she hugged me and her hand massaged my shoulder, "This was certainly a splendid idea. Whatever made you think of it? My favorite dessert. Peaches go so well with plain ol' ice cream, don't they?"

"I just knew you liked it," I shrugged, then smiled, finished off my bowl, and figured that Aunt Anne's vulnerability was an endearing asset that made me love her even more.

Sweet Peas and Apricots

The highway down the big hill from the east
gave two gifts in summer:
wild sweet peas and apricots.
The road curved like a hairpin near the top,
and in late June there would appear jumbled masses
of brilliant, fuchsia, sweet peas,
tumbling out of the roadside ditch.
We looked for their blooming each summer,
hoping that they hadn't winterkilled,
still there to take our breath away.

As if not to be outdone,
in July the second curve
was yellow with apricots.
Some were spoiled by car wheels,
some warmed on the asphalt and along the shoulder,
all waiting to be eaten,
scooped into pockets and lunch bags,
turned into jam.

The tree, oversized and old,
was a weighted riot of golden summer fruit
an offering of refreshment,
a reason to dawdle,
an August respite on the steep climb home.

Floyd and Laurel

"I'M GOING TO HELP THE GIRLS DO DISHES," I SAID, ALREADY halfway out the kitchen door.

"Go then," Aunt Mary replied, pretending a *poor me* and waving her dish cloth in the air behind me. "I'll do the rest—here, all by myself."

With little guilt, I left, tore down the front steps to the road, across the wide front lawn of the hotel, and entered through the back screen door. The kitchen was hot with steam and fragrant with the smell of food on trays ready to be served. My presence and conversation with my chums Evie, Grace and Joyce Knudson and the other waitresses, all of whom had jobs to do, was disruptive. It broke the rhythm of serving, scraping, and washing, and I was reminded by Floyd Knudson, the owner, that if I was going to stay, I'd better grab a towel and get to work. How much more fun it was wiping dishes there than wiping them at home!

"Sh-s-sh. Stop the noise, girls!" admonished Floyd's wife Laurel, when we got a little too rambunctious. "People are still eating their dessert in there. We can't have all this noise in the kitchen." She was elbow-deep in a sink filled with dishes, pots, and pans, and until the Health Department passed a regulation mandating dishwashers, they were done by hand.

Floyd was a great tease but saw to it that everybody stuck to business. A white butcher's apron was tied around his stocky, muscular frame, and even as he made the gravy and dished up Sunday chicken, I could see his large biceps flexing as he gripped the spoons. Although he joked with us continually and did his best to embarrass us, he nevertheless kept an ear out as to what was going on with all "his girls" and the older waitresses as well.

"Ya, sure," he'd say, sucking in his words in imitation of Norsk and grinning, "I betcha got a heavy date tonight? Lookin' for a little squeezin'? Watch that hand on the knee. Just a little tickle, eh?" We all would giggle, and Floyd would finish with a "heh, heh."

"Flo-oyd," Laurel would respond half-seriously, "now that's enough now."

Floyd teased us about growing up, snapped our fannies with wet towels, and let us pick leftovers in the pan. Sometimes he'd grab us and squeeze us hard. In his grip there wasn't any wiggle room and no doubt that he was boss, either. Everyone who knew Floyd loved and respected him for his good humor, intelligence and tenacity.

When I first met Laurel Knudson, she was canning tomatoes, holding a newborn in one arm and stuffing the fruit into Mason jars with the other. What I noticed most about her were the dark circles under her eyes and how tired she looked. The Knudsons had lived just up the road from us at the top of the Big Hill, and as there were no other children nearby, my aunts thought the girls, Joyce, Grace and Evie, so close to my age, would make perfect playmates. To the east of their house were two small cabins whose bedrooms were divided with curtains or partitions instead of walls. The girls were charged with keeping them clean in addition to weeding the vegetable garden. Grace, Joyce, and Evie all had to take turns weeding, a task I detested with all my heart. So I had great empathy for

Evie when her dad, Floyd told her, "No, you're not finished yet! You finish hoeing those two rows."

"No! I'm not going to do it," she cried, pleading to be let off. Floyd wouldn't tolerate back talk and licked her hard. I thought he was cruel and watched my step from then on.

What I didn't know was that Floyd and Laurel were saving hard to purchase a hotel down in the village. Growing food and canning were just samples of the hard work that was to come. Fortunately for me, my aunts decided to purchase a house of their very own closer into town, soon after Floyd and Laurel had purchased the old, huge, rambling building which happened to be right next door to our newly acquired residence. But when I saw the hotel's dingy, gray windows and the rundown interior for the first time, my heart sank. I was certain it was haunted and filled with bats. "Tell your mom and dad," I warned Grace, "no one will stay in a place like this! They can never fix it up. Your folks are gonna lose all their money, and then you'll have to move away."

Everything in the hotel needed cleaning, redoing, and replacing. By the next summer, Floyd had painted the entire exterior, which must have been the equivalent of six or seven houses. He'd painted the floors, the walls, and the ceilings of the majority of bedrooms upstairs, too. The living room had been painted, the dining room wallpapered, floors sanded and refinished, and the kitchen redone in Scandinavian yellow and blue. He had done it by himself while holding down another job beside. "That Floyd," everybody said. "He's a bear for work!"

In addition to all he accomplished at the hotel, he closed up our cabin and numerous others, shut off the water, drained pipes, and kept an eye out for damage over the winter. "We'll have to ask Floyd," we said when things went wrong at our house, and soon the fixing was arranged.

Each spring, the hotel was a fresh revelation of his monumental efforts. Bathrooms were added in almost every room. A cottage on the front lawn of the hotel was torn down, the old lawn leveled, and several new cottages built behind the hotel. From the road to the front steps of the building, he laid a flagstone walk of close to a hundred feet and bordered it with brilliant ribbons of petunias on each side. Floyd loved gardens. Cabins on the shore across the road were all remodeled, and a cement pier and shelter house was built for swimmers and sunset enthusiasts. His last big project was a large TV room constructed without the use of any power tools.

Before roads on the peninsula were asphalted, they were made of crushed rock. One of Floyd's early jobs was splitting the rock and feeding it to a crusher After a day's work heaving rocks, he told me, he came home at night with bloody hands. The limestone was so rough, it took the skin right off the fingers, and gloves wore out in no time. But during the Depression years, work was scarce and people took whatever jobs were available. During The War, and like many other men in the area, Floyd worked in the shipyards. He helped his father in the cherry orchard, took on any odd job, and through the years, suffered through hard winters and numerous hard times.

But there was a vulnerable softness in his rugged character and one felt safe just being around him. When he laughed, it was a laughter that bubbled from his heart. Lacking much formal education, he made up for it with brains, determination, and strong hands that never stopped moving. Floyd's features didn't set him off as being handsome, but his smile certainly did, and it underscored the feeling that here was a man who understood his own self-worth.

Laurel's summers were exhausting, with four girls and guests to care for, laundry to do, and hot stoves over which to labor. She mended, made pies, planned, baked rolls, washed dishes, answered phones, and took reservations. When the dishes were done, she went to the hotel living room and visited with guests, a perennial hostess to their needs and whims, and stayed awake until most guests were in and settled for the night. At the crack of dawn, both Floyd and Laurel were up again, manning the wood stoves and turning sausages, a routine they repeated every day until fall.

But even then, Laurel wasn't finished. The hotel had to be closed for the winter and there was decorating to be done, curtains to be sewn, and Christmas cards to be written and mailed to former guests. In no time, it was spring again. I marveled at her patience and endurance, her consistent generosity to everyone, and I wondered how she could be so many things for so many people. But caring seemed to come naturally to her, and compassion was written in her eyes. She was one of those women who gave the full measure of herself with little complaint.

Throughout the summer, I almost lived at the hotel and was treated as if I belonged there. Each spring when I returned and stuck my head around the kitchen door, I was made to feel as if I had never been away. And it was true. I never really left them in the fall because I spent all winter thinking of them. Not once did either Floyd or Laurel tell me to, "Go home," though I am sure Floyd would have liked to paddle me sometimes.

I was thankful he wasn't around the day Evie wore her new pair of tennis shoes. They had white soles and the canvas tops were so beautifully red that she had a hard time keeping her eyes off of them. I asked Laurel if Evie could play and then teased my friend into taking a walk to break those shoes in. We sauntered along the sandy beach most of the way, but toward the end, the sand became rough from stones that had tumbled from the bluff to the shore below. Evie looked down at her new shoes and saw that the rubber around the edge was loosening. "It's ruining my shoes," she complained. "Creen, Creen, I want to go home."

"Sissy," I said, "come on! I thought you said you'd come with me." By the time we met Laurel in the kitchen, the shoes were nearly ruined. Tears welled in Laurel's eyes. "Those are your good summer shoes," she admonished in complete frustration as she kneaded dough. "That's all you get all summer." Evie was blamed for ruining her shoes, but it was my fault, and Laurel knew it. After I was old enough to understand the struggle of those beginning years, I hoped she'd forgiven me for what I'd done.

It is strange that when one thinks about who is or is not successful in life, success is often measured in terms of corporate or academic achievement. These "high achievers" are often narrowly focused, however. Floyd could do everything, and I was certain that if he were to be stranded on a deserted island, he would likely find a way to survive, perhaps comfortably. Nowadays few men could. Floyd was a builder, and Laurel provided the material to hold things together.

What defines the land as a place to be recalled, revered? What gives it soul and softness? Quiet now, through with their building, it is those individuals who fit no mold who define it. Those who gave so freely, still are giving, defining what being means, even under the stones that mark their ends.

Rocks

THE GREAT BLUFF OF LAYERED LIMESTONE, HEAVED FROM AN ancient sea, was a towering bulkhead viewed across the bay. It was testament to the mighty glacial forces that eleven-thousand years ago gouged and scoured the peninsula into its many bays and cliffs. Had we been aboriginal, we might have reverenced our view with sacrifices. Instead, artists sat on the shore with paper and brush and painted. Those who were less artistic simply looked, sucked in the fresh breeze blowing across the water from the west, etched the whole vision in their heads, and held the power of it as closely as they could.

Our side of the bay contained white patches of sand. Sand graduated to boulders, then tables of fallen rock as the shoreline finally curved northward, the rugged cliffs of that opposing peninsula defining the harbor. Our populated eastern bluff was gentler. White houses and church steeples were scattered around the water's edge and strung across rocky ledges blanketed by trees. On the most northeastern edge of the bay, cedars grew to the water's edge and leaned wildly toward the lake like tipping building cranes.

Living with so many rocks necessitated moving them. For

years, farmers had removed them from their fields and built stone fence lines that outlined perimeters of fields and garden plots. Before asphalt roads, rock was blasted from local quarries and reduced to gravel for the road through town. It was back-breaking, dangerous work, (the old man who caned our kitchen chairs and had lost his eyesight in a blasting accident was evidence of that). Roads were costly. Fireplaces and foundations were rock, as were stepping stones, stairs, walls, and benches. Rock characterized every open space, every secret place, and yard. It dulled hoes and bent the spading forks of anyone who wished to shape the wildness. Huge limestone slabs, too large to be lifted, lay on the ground like banquet tables, providing resting places for squirrels and birds, and brief landing fields for red dragon flies and cobalt blue darning needles. They also became convenient cutting boards for fishermen who cleaned their catch for the finality of skillets.

I watched Aunt Mary clean my fish, bending over the large flat rock wedged between two trees in back of the house. She severed heads and tails of my small perch, slit the flesh along the dorsal fin and peeled away the scales and skin. But, she soon tired of cleaning my almost daily catch and entrusted her favorite, sharpest blade to me. "You clean them and then I'll cook them," she said.

I grew expert at it. At different times of the year, the fish ate different things: flies, small crabs, and minnows. I could examine my partially digested worm. I could distinguish livers, hearts, galls, and marvel at the efficiency of gills for breathing. Sometimes as I skinned them, a reflex action of their nerves made the white flesh twitch and the bodies contort. Aunt Mary begged me to wait until the fish were completely dead before I cleaned them. Each summer, indentations on the stone table multiplied as my knife tore through the spines of hundreds of perch and ground the soft limestone into powder fine enough for faces. That stone was mine, I thought, and I would clean my fish on it forever. I could not leave that house because I could not move that stone.

In front of the house was a stone wall stacked high with fossilized coral stands, brachiopods, trilobites, and scallop shells. Our wall was history. Fossil souvenir hunters scoured fieldstone piles all over the peninsula looking for such stones and carried them home for door stops, paperweights, and decorations. Scattered in unconnected places, Georgia, Mississippi, Illinois, and Indiana, the best examples were lost forever, and still may be collecting dust on windowsills.

In spring after Aunt Anne's garden was dug, my job was removing the rocks heaved up each year by winter frost to make hoeing easier. Each morning, I was told to fill five pails and dump them in a pile next to the woods. After several days, I rebelled. "It's cruel to make children pick rocks," I protested. "Barbaric." I stamped my foot. I cried. Nevertheless, they were insistent about it, and I was forbidden to do anything else until I had complied.

Large stones were the first picked up, but as the spring wore on, the succeeding pails filled up with the smaller ones. That meant more bending, and the pails grew heavier and heavier. I threatened to tell the whole world that I was made to carry rocks. I described the prison chain gang in a movie I had seen. But I was only reminded that if I liked Aunt Anne's garden peas, if I liked creamed new potatoes with veal cooked in sour cream, or lovely beet greens soaked in butter, then I had better earn my keep and carry rocks. When the peas began to bear and the first tiny red potatoes were dug, my ordeal ended for the summer, but my resentment simmered.

It resurfaced every time I washed my socks. We didn't have a washing machine. Our sheets and towels were sent to the laundry. Because of the expense, the rest we washed by hand. But keeping white socks white wasn't easy. I scrubbed and bleached them in a pail balanced on the stone wall in the back yard and used rocks as a convenient washboard. Each rub reminded me of picking stones.

I have a rock on the windowsill in my living room. It is a jumbled mass of brachiopods. Another displays an excellent stand of coral. But, these are more than stones. They are the bluff and the wind that blew over it, the cutting board wedged between birch trees and the smell of perch and cornmeal browning in sweet oil in the skillet. They are Aunt Anne hoeing her garden, edible pod peas with veal cooked in sour cream with delicate new potatoes, and being trusted to clean my own fish. These are disconnected flickerings of the mind, too complicated even for computers.

Housekeepers

NEVER ENOUGH MONEY. THERE WERE ICE CREAM CONES AND chocolate Cokes to buy at the ice cream parlor. Sometimes a hot fudge sundae—and the juke box, too! Hellgrammites for the early bass season, Wednesday night movies at the Village Hall, and Aunt Mary's July birthday present. In addition, I enjoyed renting a rowboat when I wished (a mere quarter an hour) and wanted to save up for a hand-crafted silver ring with my initial on it.

I decided to ask Laurel if she needed help. After all, each time I asked Evie, Grace, or Joyce if they could play, she'd say, "Not right now, Corinne. They have jobs to do. Come back around 1:00 or 2:00. We have a hotel to run, you know!"

"I'll help my friends make beds!" I reasoned, knowing I was too young to be paid for many other jobs. Their work would be finished faster, and I would ask for such little pay, it was unlikely they could refuse. "Please, Ple-ea-se," I pleaded with their mother. "You won't be sorry. You won't have to pay me much, maybe like a quarter or fifty cents a day? I promise I'll do a good job. Please?"

"Well, we'll think about it," Laurel answered. "We don't

pay the girls much, you know. It's not easy starting out. Hard paying anybody."

"When will you let me know?" I kept on, hoping not to be put off. "I know the girls won't mind. We'll have fun making beds."

"We'll see," replied Laurel, elbow deep in dough for the dinner rolls to be served that evening.

Each morning, I checked to determine when the girls could play and asked again, "Have you decided yet? Well, when do you think you will decide? Tomorrow? The end of the week? Could we just try it once?"

"I think I may have a job," I told my aunts one morning as they sat in the living room. Aunt Helen put her knitting down.

"Doing what?"

"Cleaning rooms and making beds with the girls," I answered blithely.

"And, young lady," interjected Aunt Mary with an unusually serious expression, "what do you think your mother will say when she comes up here and finds her daughter is a housemaid? Are you sure that's something you really want to do?"

Aunt Anne, always champion of the underdog, took my side. "There's nothing wrong with that kind of work," she said emphatically. "I think it would be good experience for her."

Still, I had to ask my mother first. I decided to call home. If she heard my voice, it would be easier to convince her. Besides, letters took too long, and in the meantime, I could be making money. However, it was an idea I knew Mother would have trouble with. Her daughter cleaning someone else's room! With the charges reversed from the phone at the hotel, I begged and begged until she finally said with a sigh of resignation, "I don't suppose there's much I can do about it. If I say no, you'll go ahead and do it anyway. I'll just have to depend on your Auntie Waltons' judgment."

Victoriously, and with the vision of coins in my pocket, I returned to the house and announced to my aunts that, just as I knew she would from the beginning, "Mother said I could."

Yet, all this discussion I decided was somewhat of a game on my aunts' part, and I sensed they secretly enjoyed their role in the outcome, finding it, in fact, amusing. Laurel at last agreed also, and for the several weeks the job lasted, my mornings were spent scouring sinks in the large communal bathroom at the end of the hall, dusting dressers, and mopping under beds.

The dirty sheets were piled in the upstairs hotel hallway then quickly swept away to the laundry. In those beginning years when money was tight, expensive sheets were in short supply. Often, they were barely dry before a bed had to be remade. We began about nine, working down the hall as guests checked out or left for the morning. Laurel spent a good portion of her time washing linens to save the cost of having them done commercially. Along with taking care of the individual needs of her own family, she took reservations, answered the phone, oversaw the kitchen, visited with guests until late at night, and sank into her bed exhausted, not caring whether her own bedroom was picked up and dusted or her own sheets changed. Sometimes, in the middle of the night, she and Floyd were called to nurse a sick guest or search for lost keys. Nevertheless, they still had to be ready at 5:00 in the morning to prepare breakfast. The frequent sighs in Laurel's voice as she spoke and the weary expression in her eyes, left little doubt that she was a monument to the resilience of the human spirit.

The hotel's exterior was white wooden clapboard. A long, pillared porch stretched across the front and, in the middle, wooden steps and a large trumpet vine welcomed guests to the front office. The third floor was seldom used after the hotel opened because of fire insurance regulations. Wooden steps in the back and on the side of the building provided access for housekeepers, and from the twenty or twenty-five-foot-high landings, we shook mops and bundled the accumulated laundry from each floor. Those landings provided such a commanding view of the bay that it was hard not to have a few doubts about the wisdom of work and the necessity of money.

When the hotel was first purchased, the original furniture came with it. The rooms were sparsely furnished and barely adequate for an increasingly demanding public. Also, they were in desperate need of painting the first year or two. The bedroom floors were made of wide pine boards, and despite coats of fresh gray paint, were rough enough to snag dust mops and make cleaning a frustration. Furnishings were antique. Old dressers were draped with dresser scarves and a bowl and water pitcher sat on the top. In some rooms there was a matching thunder mug on the floor near the dresser, meant for emergency use only, since the previous hotel owner had

installed a single large bathroom at the end of the hall. Closet space was almost nonexistent. The beds were wrought iron, the bedspreads white cotton. Thin, sill-length, gauzy curtains let the sunlight and lake breeze flow freely through the rooms, and window shades with string pulls and finger circles provided privacy from below. Several cotton throw rugs were placed about the room, and an old mirror hung above each dresser.

With few exceptions, most single guests were women. During the summer I "worked," however, a bachelor on the second floor was one of those exceptions. The scruffy, unkempt, little old man with several days of stubble, was obviously fed up with shaving. He had arrived alone, spent much of the week alone, an seemed an enigma to everyone, although he talked a lot. An early riser, he spent little time in his room. That was more than satisfactory to us girls as it enabled us get an early start with cleaning. We made his bed, then mopped the edges of his room. But one time the mop struck something when I tried to wipe under the bed frame. Perplexed, I got down on all fours to see. "A thunder mug! Now why would he put it under there?" I complained, reaching way under to pull it out. As it slid toward me I sensed liquid moving in it. The three of us whooped and gagged when we removed the cover, caught the retch inducing stench of stale urine, and quickly replaced the lid as rapidly as possible. We "ished" and held our noses, for that thunder mug must have contained a week's worth of accumulated urine and WE had to dump it!

"Just like him," Evie emphasized. "Inconsiderate! Yuk! Why couldn't he have dumped it himself?"

"He's only three doors from the toilet!" Grace complained incredulously, her face screwed up as if she were about to vomit. "Just wait 'til I tell Momma!"

But as cleaners and bed makers, our view through a keyhole gave us most to talk about the rest of the summer. It was rather late in the morning and one door in the hallway was still closed. Usually, we knew who had left for the day but always knocked first just in case. If there were no answer, the door was opened with the large antique skeleton key, and then we'd quickly tidy up the room. Grace said she hadn't seen the couple that morning at breakfast, but it was already so late that we all assumed the guests must be out. A gentle knock on their door produced no response and a twist of the milk glass door knob indicated the door was locked. "Maybe they're dead in there," Grace laughed as she peeked through the key hole to check things out. She looked intently through the hole for several seconds and then motioned for me to take over. "Evie! Evie!" one of us whispered, waving a hand, beckoning her from the room on the other side of the hall. Soon we were all peeking.

The naked couple were passionately entwined, kissing and feeling each other's bodies as they half-sat, half-laid on the edge of the bed. I hardly knew what was occurring, having had no experience by which to process what I saw, and so stared dumbfounded and embarrassed but magnetized by the microscopic view. Joyce had to see this, and we went to get her.

"Joyce! Come look! You've got to see what they're doing."

Joyce was busy in the last room at the end of the hall and left her sheets to see what this was all about. She crouched down to peer through the key hole, also. "What are they doing that for, Joyce?" we questioned, "It's such a beautiful day, why do they want to stay up here all morning? Why don't they go outside and do something."

Then, Joyce stood up and motioned emphatically for us to get away from the door!

"That's the newlyweds. They just got in last night," she informed us smugly, with the all-knowing look older sisters muster when they want to. Evie, Grace, and I took a final look and then, in our embarrassment, pulled away. The rest of the beds were made without much conversation. We were digesting. What we had seen was discussed and tittered over for several summers. "Remember the newlyweds?" we'd recall later with a smile.

"You should have seen them," I told my aunts excitedly. "They were on the edge of the bed without any clothes on and they were kissing each other!" Not long after that, my aunts talked to Mrs. Irmanetta who owned a cherry orchard besides growing strawberries, raspberries, and boysenberries, which would soon be ripe. I picked them, sometimes with Evie and Grace, who got a reprieve from bed making, except on rainy days. The honeymooners didn't stay long, so I didn't get to see what they really looked like. More than likely, I wouldn't have recognized them anyway, and because they'd behaved so strangely, probably wouldn't have liked them very much.

Captain Green

Captain Green, I was told, had sailed Clipper ships on the Atlantic, but in his later years, sailed with the last of the clippers on the Great Lakes. The thought of living a life such as his was the stuff of my most intense imaginings and dreams, so much so that I felt cursed not to have been born into the age of the great ships. Additionally, I was trapped in the body of a girl without any possibility of escape. I wanted freedom to work on a boat, even an ore boat. I wanted to spit two feet out and have it be all right because I was a man! I had watched ore boats, pencil lines against the horizon, inching their way from one edge of my dream to the other.

"Hell," I'd tell them, "give me the damn rope. I'll tie 'er down. Don't mess with me, Buster, or I'll knock your blinkin' head into next week."

To the sea in ships. In bed at night, I planned. Buzz off my hair, brown in the sun, callous my hands—perhaps they'd take me. But I would always have to wear a tee shirt, although some men did have semblances of breasts and mine were small. A bunk mate? Could he be sworn to secrecy? And what about the showers? If I worked long and hard, as well as any man, being

discovered might not make much difference. They'd keep me anyway. Then, the disappointment of being born all wrong would come again. It was some mistake. My spirit wasn't female. Life would be spent wishing. Pretending.

The dream didn't go away. I worked and ate, spit and showered on those ore boats often. I tramped the welded metal squares of decking, wound ropes on cleats and rusty winches, rode out storms and slid through hours of mist with fog horns moaning. I sweated in the sunlight of July and August, moved cargo, ate meals with mates, and laughed over breaded pork and mashed potatoes in the galley. It was the romantic call of the sea I felt, and more than anything, I wanted to meet the Captain before he died. I wanted to tell him that I could sail and splice rope, too, and that even though I was a girl, I was just as tough as he had been. I wanted to hear all the tales about terrible storms, of life on a ship, and know what the men he sailed with were like. I wanted to see how weathered his face was and get a good look at the gnarled hands that had pulled so much rope and raised so many sails. I wanted to know if he still imagined clippers on the horizon, if he dreamed about his past life and wished he could live it all over again. However, Captain Green was up in years and had become something of a recluse. I had no idea where he lived and had never even seen him at the post office.

It was early in the season on a cool and clouded morning when my friend, Grace, pointed him out to me. He was walking slowly with the aid of a cane along the roadside and was headed down to the docks to meet a couple of cronies from the village. Several of the local oldtimers often frittered away their mornings, swinging their feet back and forth against the cement floor of Thorp's boat house, talking about the past and gossiping about nothing. As soon as I realized that this was my chance to meet the Captain, all thoughts of other morning activities were set aside and I raced down the flagstone walk by brilliant pink petunias to catch up to him and walk beside him into town.

Curiously, he didn't look like a sea captain, although I had no reason to expect him to look differently than anybody else. He wore an old green cap with visor and a ragged wool sports jacket which hung misshapenly over his bent shoulders.

"Hi," I said, "Are you Captain Green? Did you used to sail clipper ships?" I fell in along side of him, scuffing the gravel at the edge of the road with the toes of my tennis shoes.

"Sometimes," he replied. I skipped a little in my excitement, expecting he'd ask me who I was or where I lived, or if I sailed myself or something. But he did not.

"Those must have been romantic times," I continued with a sigh, expecting him to understand my yearning to sail ships like the men I'd read about in books and seen in "Yachting Magazine."

"It was a job," he said matter-of-factly. "Just a job." He was quite unresponsive. Despite my obvious enthusiasm, his conversation was sparse, and there were accompanying lengthy pauses between my questions and his answers.

"Don't you miss it? Don't you ever wish you could sail 'em again?" I continued, determined to tease something of interest from him.

"Nope," he said matter-of-factly again.

"How come? How could you not miss it. I mean, isn't it in your blood? Isn't it hard to live on land?"

"I like land better. Should have been a farmer instead," he responded almost as if he were wishing me away.

The Captain was not what I expected. Not only did he not look like a sailor, he didn't even talk like one! I'd read John Masefield's, "Sea Fever" and I knew the sea was really in that author's bones. When he wrote about "the wheel's kick and the wind's song and the white sail's shaking… and the flung spray and the blown spume and the sea gulls crying," it was so powerful, so compelling that the Queen of England made him Poet Laureate, and I could actually feel the spray of the ocean on my face.

Captain Green had spoiled the poem and the sea, and I was suddenly angry with him for it. The dream of hearing yarns from a true sailor, one of the last of the breed, was shattered. He was just an ordinary old man who at one time had read the clouds but never marveled at them, who'd felt the crisp air over the water, but I guessed that he had never really smelled it. He wasn't worthy of The Poet Laureate's musings, I surmised. I left him and walked back to my friends at the hotel without the grace of any understanding.

My mother, Nellie Bliss Dickerson,
circa 1943, soon after
she began working

Anne, Mary and Helen Walton
circa 1955

The Oshkoshers: Catherine Joslyn on left, Mildred Leyda on right.
Fishing at the coal dock, Sister Bay, Wisconsin, 1954

Village Hall/Post Office,
circa 1945–50

Kitchen, Evergreen Beach Hotel,
Ephraim, Wisconsin
L–R in back: waitresses Bonnie, Sue and Ellen with Joyce Knudson
Front L–R: Floyd, Evie and Laurel Knudson, circa 1960

Grace, Corinne and Joyce,
on the front lawn of
Evergreen Beach Hotel
circa 1950–55

Wilson's Ice Cream Parlor,
circa 1945–50

Aunt Kit and the Good Humor Man

LIKE CLOCKWORK, AUNT KIT AND UNCLE WILL MCEVOY arrived in July for a two-week visit. We waited in the car for the bus to drop them off sometime between 5:00 and 6:00 in the afternoon in front of Evergreen Beach Hotel. It was a vacation they anticipated all winter long. Uncle Will dreamed of meeting last year's fishing friends again and someone new to whom he could tell well-worn jokes. For Aunt Kit, it was a pleasure just to have a little relief from hot summers in Chicago's inner city, to relax, reminisce, and share time once more with her old high school chums, my aunties, who considered Aunt Kit more like another sister than a mere friend. But neither could have been more excited about their visit than I, for the world I lived in was one of women and few men.

Aunt Kit was delightfully tolerant, witty, and humorously cynical. All of us considered her something of a saint, for although Uncle Will was a wonderful man, he was a modest provider and repeated the same old jokes so many times, one felt only a seraph could have survived it. Aunt Kit, however, listened and laughed as if she were hearing those jokes for the first time. I watched her repeat this performance with the same accomplished skill for two weeks every year in summer. She was a petite woman, though broad of beam, and the silk print dresses she had sewn with such expertise, draped comfortably over her wide hips. I liked not having her too perfect. She and my aunts would sit visiting by the hour the first few days after their arrival, all similarly groomed, and from my vantage place on the floor, their sturdy, laced black oxford walking shoes defined the chair arrangement in the living room.

Uncle Will and I did other things. Aunt Helen prepared sandwiches and drove us to the dock where we spent mornings and afternoons fishing instead. He always called me, "Darlin,'" and his cheerful Irish brogue and kindness endeared him to me and most everyone. I thought of him as a rather simple man, but interestingly, something about him far outshone the more intellectual men I knew. In fact, they often sought him out, perhaps because of his vivacious, straightforward, and light-hearted nature, which one sensed masked something deeper.

Not a handsome man, he was of moderate height and build, with a few wisps of white hair strung over his sunburned head. His features were rather coarse and his nose a little large and slightly red, although he seldom drank even a glass of wine. But his laugh was purely honest and infectious, and I decided early in our relationship that he was a treasure. During the winter, he worked in the Chicago Post Office. In the summer, he was also an umpire at Wrigley Field. He couldn't get enough of baseball and had baseball jokes, along with a host of others, he related, though none were even slightly off-color. It was the Oshkosh girls who told him the shady ones, and when the four of us fished together, we were accompanied by a never-ending stream of laughter.

Uncle Will and I became very close over the years. I was of Scottish descent and had read somewhere that the Scots were Irish marauders. I signed my winter letters to him Corinne McBliss, and sent him potatoes dyed green for St. Patrick's Day, along with green candles. Choosing potatoes that sat level on the table, I cored a hole in each to make a candle holder and stuffed the shipping box with Irish poems, Erin Go Braugh pins, and paper shamrocks. Once, I drew a map of Ireland, painted it green and white, and defined and titled counties and towns in gold paint. The entire map was glued to plywood and cut into a jigsaw puzzle. My gifts and his replies were preludes to our coming summer together.

Aunt Kit also had her stories to tell. Theirs was a marriage which I thought of as ideal, the kind most likely "made in heaven." With her sharp-tongued good humor, she made Will tow the mark and he seemed to enjoy every bit of it, evidenced by Aunt Kit's repetition of "The Duck Story" year after year and his ability to laugh over that tale at his own expense.

"Before Will worked for the post office," she would begin, "he was an oldtime semipro pitcher and played at Logan Square Ball Park, which was close to our Chicago flat. The team was good enough to beat the Cubs and the Chicago White Sox in September after the Big League season closed. After all that pitching and tossing of mail into open bags at the post office, Will's pitch was pretty accurate," Aunt Kit said as she'd flash a mischievous smile, "and duck soup for Will.

"The Polish National Alliance was running a carnival at the park as a fundraiser, which included a number of games of chance. One booth required throwing three balls into a bucket from a distance of about twenty feet—the prize if all three balls made it was a live duck. Uncle Will easily pitched in three balls and won a duck for only ten cents. Then a little old lady with a Polish accent nudged him. She had seen his success and asked him determinedly, 'You get me a duck too, Mister?'

The next three balls made the bucket, so a second duck was handed over for a dime. Soon, friends of the little old lady got wind of ducks for only ten cents, and the concession lost four more ducks in only fifteen minutes. By now, the carny was getting perturbed, as the loss of any more ducks would put him out of business. 'Beat it, you,' he finally snarled at Uncle Will, 'before I run out of ducks!'"

All of this occurred on a Saturday night, and as Aunt Kit had everything prepared for Sunday dinner, something had to be done with the duck. The back porch of their flat was enclosed by a railing and although the floor had been scrubbed down that day, "Mr. Duck," as Aunt Kit told it, "was tied by one leg to a post and left there."

Uncle Will slept late on Sundays, as in the afternoon, he umpired semipro ballgames. But Aunt Kit was always up by sunrise, and at 7:30 entered their bedroom and shouted to Uncle Will, "Get up and get that G.D. duck off the porch! The floor's been whitewashed already!"

"I don't know what to do with it," Will retorted. Aunt Kit's stiletto reply was rapid and determined.

"Take him over to the kosher butcher and execute him!" she demanded.

So Will dressed and soon was on his way down the alley with the live duck under his arm. About ten minutes later, however, as Aunt Kit stood on the back porch, cleaning it for the second time, she saw him returning with the duck still alive and squawking.

She railed at him from the third floor porch, "What goes on? Did the duck get a stay of execution?"

"And your Unc shouted back to me," she'd say chuckling, "The kosher butcher won't kill the duck until the Rabbi returns from the temple!"

"Take that duck back," Aunt Kit ordered loudly, "and either wait there for the Rabbi or call the Priest for yourself because one of you is going to get killed!!"

Aunt Kit said the duck was eventually cooked, but it was as tough as a rubber boot and just as easy to cut. "In fact," she continued, "you couldn't have cut it with an ax!"

Uncle Will and Aunt Kit brought us laughter over a period of many years and continued to visit my one remaining Walton aunt until the last of their generation aged, exchanged summer cottages for nursing homes, and replayed the laughter in the silence of their little rooms.

Berries

EACH SPRING, SMALL WHITE BLOSSOMS SNUGGLING CLOSE TO the ground presaged the season of strawberry fruiting. If there was ever a bit of land that produced raspberries, boysenberries, or strawberries that were any sweeter or any larger, I hadn't heard of it. Sometimes my aunts picked strawberries and brought home baskets of the mammoth things for cold strawberry pies, short cake, angel foods hollowed and filled with mashed berries and whipped cream, jam making, or ordinary smothered ice cream. Often, we took the biggest by their stems, dipped them first in port or sherry, then in powdered sugar, and tipping our heads backward to ensure not a drop escaped us, devoured them whole in a scarlet Bacchanalian feast.

Certainly the soil had something to do with their sweetness, as perhaps did cool nights and the extended springs. Maybe it was reward for struggling in the soil in which they grew, persisting against odds without modern chemical fertilizers. This was the season to hope for the rain that ensured a bountiful berry crop, and it nearly always came plentifully in June.

Late in the month of June and early in July, wild strawberries made the meadows where they grew rosy with color. Low, sparse vegetation struggling through the rocky meadows diffused the red with soft green and the gold of withered grasses from the year before. Laurel gave us kettles and we set out to pick, the idea of wild strawberry jam burning in our brains. There were two types of berries: one with a fruit small and elongated, the other round, much denser and with firmer flesh. By the time the bottom of the pail was covered, our lower backs were aching. We had had enough. Any ideas I had about subsistence survival on summer berries if the Germans came and cut us off had faded. Our hands were red with juice and our mouths awash with the lingering flavor of precious fruit.

The other side of the peninsula was swept by Lake Michigan winds. The soil was sandier, more exposed, and poorer than in the field close to our house. Yet, years later, still in the habit of picking, I discovered there the largest wild

berries I had ever seen. They were round and sweet, with the perfection of flavor like that of summer vegetables gathered just before frost comes. I picked a pan full of them and made jam.

In the rocky meadows berries quickly disappeared, the reddish leaves turned golden and, as if in desperation, fringed themselves with burgundy. But the field would not be forgotten. For, later and without warning, the hawk weed bloomed. As if ignited, it seemed a firey red and yellow carpet; consuming the field, contrasting dark trunks of maples at its southern edge, stealing the show, drawing applause. It was an empathic gift of Nature. A flashing substitute for jam.

Worms

EVIE AND GRACE DIDN'T FISH, SO THEY HAD NO NEED FOR worms. Nevertheless, we spent many evenings catching night crawlers together on the front lawn of the hotel until late at night, merely because it was fun. With a flashlight in one hand and a coffee can in the other, it was hard not to become giggly after an hour or two of bending and grabbing. The sounds of our voices carried all over the hotel grounds and right into the open bedroom windows of the second floor. "Corinne! Corinne!" Grace called in an excited, mock whisper, beckoning us to move in her direction. "Over here. Under the apple tree. They're ALL over!"

"You walked all over my spot," Evie whined as I tip toed across the grass toward Grace. "It'll be another fifteen minutes before they come out again, now!"

"I didn't walk on it! Go pick someplace else then. There're enough worms around for everybody. Hey! Now don't come over here and spoil mine!"

"Shu-shh, girls," Laurel pleaded as she stood in her nightgown at the end of the long front porch. "All the guests are sleeping! I want to go to bed. I'm tired. Haven't you gotten enough of that yet?" Laurel had no intention of spoiling our fun, but she didn't want to have guests complaining the next morning about having had their sleep interrupted either.

Catching night crawlers was an addictive pastime. Each looked bigger than the last one, and until our backs felt as if they were going to break in two, there was just no possibility of stopping. The beams from our flashlights bobbed up and down and around the yard for hours. Flashlights were as much of a necessity for catching worms in the grass as they were in the house for locating candles in kitchen drawers during a storm or finding the way to the bathroom on a black night. We used them hour after hour in late June, July, and August. I bought lots of batteries over the summer.

Floyd watered the hotel lawn and the petunia bed bordering the sides of the flagstone walk, particularly when dry weather arrived in August, and soon after dusk, worms began to appear. They wove themselves through the wet blades of grass and lay stretched out, glistening and vulnerable, throughout the petunia bed and all over the lawn. If I remained still enough and didn't startle them with too much light, I could watch them emerge from a little mound of dirt, wave to and fro in search of a mate, and finally lie coupled by the hour, numbly engrossed in a strange hermaphroditic entanglement.

There is a trick to outsmarting worms. If the light shines on them directly, they retreat in an instant, so the flashlight can never be directed downward, but has to be played over the ground quickly at an angle instead. Identifying the telltale sheen of a crawler under the fleeting light and grabbing it before it retreats requires finesse and cunning. As soon as the worm is spotted and before it senses danger, one has to figure out which end is closest to the hole, grab that end quickly, and then pull up slowly and firmly so the worm has no chance to contract its muscles. It finally gives up and can be pulled straight out of its hole.

On perfect worming nights when they lie in pairs, two can be grabbed with one hand and two with the other, the ultimate

manifestation of worming mania! At first worms drop into the can with a dull *thunk*. But after the can begins to fill, it can be difficult to tell in the darkness if they are accidentally dangling over the edge of the can ready to wiggle to freedom, or if in our fervor, we might be missing the can altogether, dropping them onto the ground instead. Every single one was important because filling the can to the top became a goal in itself.

If anyone was still up around the hotel when we finished, sitting in the big kitchen drinking coffee and visiting, we loved to show off our night's accomplishments.

"What have you been doing out there all this time?" people asked who were unfamiliar with worming. Then we'd show them the can, full to the top. Even better was digging into the can with the hands and bringing up gobs of slimy crawlers, wiggling and dripping through the fingers. Unsettling stomachs was part of the game, too.

"My goodness! What on earth are you going to do with all of those?"

Then I could brag about the wooden crate I had back at the cottage filled with worms, how long worms lasted without rotting, and how I fed them on coffee grounds. People who sat up late in the kitchen were usually a different breed than other guests. They didn't recoil and say, "Ughhhh!" when they saw worms, and they seemed to appreciate the effort we had expended in getting them. For the remainder of their vacation, they showed an interest in how the fish were biting and how many I had caught.

If there is any virtue in worming, let alone celebrating it in writing, it is that it brings one to the realization that everything, though seemingly unrelated at first thought, actually is connected. People are connected to flashlights, flashlights to people and both to catching worms. Worms, people, and flashlights are connected to fishing and the lake, and ultimately, the excitement involved in setting a hook. Finally, there is the pleasure in consuming one's catch. And it all begins with just a flashlight and a worm! Worming establishes a relationship with the natural world in the same manner as planting seeds and later harvesting ripe fruit. In the process, one often discovers that the entire exercise has been good for the soul as well as for the appetite. That knowledge has a satisfying and inexplicably therapeutic value and enhances the pleasure of new acquaintances made because of fishing; well, really, because of worms.

Besides my pleasure over a heaping can of worms, I was proud when my catch contributed to supper. Aunt Mary always said it was a lovely string of fish and the four of us relished every mouthful when we ate them for dinner several times a week. All of that was thanks to worming, a delightful summer fever.

Worming is a diversion that can transcend age, gender, or position. When it's a perfect night for the wigglers to appear, I still feel compelled to grab a flashlight from the kitchen cupboard and a coffee can from the pantry. Braving mosquitoes in the vegetable and herb gardens, I pick worms just for the fun of it, two with one hand and two with the other. Find the right end. There. Now, pull slowly. The can is nearly full. Big bass wait tomorrow.

Mrs. Mudd

BEFORE TOURIST HORDES TOOK OVER VIRGIN TERRITORY, encounters with four-foot pine snakes were a common occurrence. They startled summer residents who aroused them from their naps on doorsteps and slithered unobtrusively through opened screen doors. They glided slowly down garden paths, sunbathed on warm flagstones, and entwined themselves around the rafters of outbuildings and tool houses, terrifying those who came upon them unexpectedly. Nowadays, the environmentally conscious person would most likely merely shoo them away, but not long ago snakes were in greater abundance and only a dedicated naturalist would have hesitated to do them in. They were chased, flayed, and hacked to death with spades and shovels with remorseless glee and that smug superiority exhibited by those who see killing as a triumph over Nature. Nearly everyone had a, "You should have seen the snake we had at our house yesterday," story to tell, but Mrs. Mudd's was by far the most stunningly graphic because of its unusual setting and circumstance.

Mrs. Mudd was an unforgettable woman for several reasons. First, she was the kind of person one liked instinctively upon first meeting. Second, she was a rather large and shapely woman, with the biggest breasts I had ever seen. When she dropped in at our house one morning to see my aunts, dressed in a white tennis outfit, I was overwhelmed with their enormity. The thought of her racing across a court and bending to return a low ball boggled my imagination.

Mrs. Mudd's summer home was in snake heaven; a dense cedar woods near the lake where stone flagstones in the walkway were continually damp with moisture. Little sun filtered in among the trees, and her cottage seemed morbidly dark and claustrophobic. In keeping with the atmosphere outside was the heavily paneled interior of the house and the brass candlesticks on her mantle, a pair of coiled cobras with erect heads and hoods spread as if prepared for a fatal strike.

One morning while sitting in her living room, Mrs. Mudd said she glanced at her mantle and thought she saw something move. It must have been her imagination, she assumed, one of those out-of-the-corner-of-the-eye tricks the mind sometimes plays.

She continued with her reading. As she glanced at the mantle a second time however, she perceived the same thing.

Hesitantly, placing her book on the table, she rose, slowly making her way to the mantle just for her own peace of mind and reassurance. Yes, everything seemed fine, except that one candlestick needed a bit of rearranging. Just as she reached to adjust it, a large pine snake the color of old tree bark began to uncoil itself from the brass stem and the cobra head. She shrieked in panic and with the blank mindless fear that accompanies sudden surges of adrenaline, dashed wildly to the next door neighbor's house for help.

The neighbor was nearly as paralyzed by the news as she was but agreed to return to Mrs. Mudd's house, armed with a broom, the longest and safest weapon readily available. When the two returned, the snake was stretched out along the mantle, and the women, breathless with fright, poked and prodded the thing until it dropped to the living room floor and slithered toward the nearby kitchen. No doubt the serpent was as terrified of their screams and the continuous jabs of the broom straws as the women were of the reptile itself. Herding the snake into the kitchen, they warded off its defensive strikes with their brooms like bullfighters heading off an angry bull with a red cape, and after an hour or so, managed to maneuver it through the back screen door.

According to Mrs. Mudd, she could never look at the mantle again without seeing that snake and lost no time in removing the candlesticks for good. (I always thought they were hideous and could never understand why anyone would grace a mantle with them in the first place.) Most people who

heard her snake story said they'd never buy or rent a cottage in woods like that so close to the lake, and remarked about how thankful they were to live exactly where they did, out in the open. Snakes, however, seemed to abound everywhere.

After that episode, I imagined snakes all over in the house. I envisioned them coiled in corners and lying motionless next to walls and baseboards in the living room. Those who had never paid much attention to their mantelpieces before eyed them carefully from then on. Back home, we only had foot-long garter snakes. But here it was was a different world, one where wildlife was more closely connected to daily life and where animals were bigger and more threatening. This was the way life really was supposed to be, I thought, and summer way up north, far away from the city, was what summers must have been like in pioneer days. I loved it!

Mrs. Mudd didn't return the following summer; not because of snakes, but because of breast cancer. Her snake story however, continued to be the best ever, especially if one enjoyed watching women and tourists recoil and shudder.

"Aren't you afraid of snakes?" visitors would say after hearing the thriller repeated in all its detail.

"Nah," I'd reply with confidence and calm, "they won't hurt ya. You should see the wood spiders I've squished in our cabin. Some of 'em are at least three inches across. Like doilies! No, I see snakes all the time and they don't bother me a bit. Ya get used to 'em. It's part of summer. Like night crawlers. Have ya ever picked night crawlers? Big, long, squishy, gooey worms?"

The Pennys

"WE'RE NOT GOING!" MR. PENNY'S EIGHT-YEAR-OLD SON hollered to his father between intermittent sobs from the bay side of the highway. "I DON'T want to go home."

Mr. Penny had just emerged from the post office to collect his mail for the last time and switch his mailing address back home. The cabin they had rented for July wasn't far from our house, and several times we had been invited there for cocktails. It was the first time my aunts had had a gin and tonic, tonic water enjoying a sudden surge in popularity at the time. They liked it, and we all liked the Pennys, too.

They had rented a cabin for a month, that month was now over, and another family was ready to arrive the next day. Their station wagon was jammed. Suitcases, fishing rods, and pillows separated the children in the back seat. Mr. Penny had parked the car opposite the post office facing south, so that as soon as he finished this last errand, they could head straight out of town toward home. A view of the automobile from the Village Hall parking lot showed the Penny's vehicle was no different than many others toward the end of the month; chassis slung low over the rear wheels and the inside stuffed to the gills with dirty clothes, bed pillows, and vacation's memorabilia.

"Don't be silly," Mr. Penny retorted with fatherly authority as he crossed the street and pointed his finger at his son. "We're going! Now get back in the car."

"No!" the boy whined. "You can leave me here." His crying suddenly became uncontrollable.

Mr. Penny was clearly frustrated and at a loss as to how to handle this embarrassing development. People emerging from the post office, soon aware of the serious altercation thanks to shouting and raised voices, began opening and reading their mail on the building's front steps or next to their cars as an excuse for not missing the finale. Perhaps they expected some revelation in the methods of handling obstreperous, unruly offspring they hadn't yet discovered.

After opening the back door for his son and repeating a few more sternly spoken "Get back in the cars," the front door on the other side of the wagon opened, and Mrs. Penny got out, soon followed by her daughter from the other side of the back seat. Now they were all crying except for Mr. Penny, suddenly confronted by his entire disconsolate family in the center of the busiest place in town.

"I don't want to go either," Mrs. Penny added, tears streaming down her cheeks, "Can't we just stay another couple weeks? Please?" The daughter stood defensively next to her mother, lending additional emphasis to the already awkward situation.

"Don't you realize I have a job?" pleaded Mr. Penny. "And besides, everything is rented," he added as an afterthought, assuming that that obvious fact would finally bring them to reality and put an end to the argument.

"How do you know?" his wife responded, desperation evident between her sobs and sniffles. "We haven't even looked! What about Mrs. Barnes' cottages? Maybe you could leave us here and come back and get us later."

The protesters momentarily cheered as they nodded in

agreement with this brilliant idea. "I can't do that." Mr. Penny responded. The tone of his voice was softer now. None of his other tactics had worked. He paused, in an evident attempt to think and gain some control over this conspiracy. People continued reading their mail. "I don't know what to say. I didn't realize you all felt that strongly about staying here."

"We do. We want to be here all summer," the boy retorted, quickly adding, "And Mom says she's never had more fun in her whole life!"

"Well, I'll tell you what," Mr. Penny sighed, in an effort to salvage a little of his self-respect in front of so many onlookers and effect any reasonable resolution to the crisis, "if you all promise to quit this nonsense and get back in the car, then I promise we'll come back sometime in August and look for a place of our own."

The two children hopped up and down and then around in circles. Mrs. Penny grabbed her husband around the neck and they kissed each other next to the station wagon, right in front of everybody. Smiles broke through their tears. The car doors quickly slammed shut, the windows were rolled down, and waving arms protruded from every side. "Goodbye," they waved, "Bye, Ephraim," and they waved as far as I could see them, around the curve of the road, until the trees obscured them from my view.

Mr. Penny became the hero of the summer season and an ideal dad, even though he'd been coerced. It was a beautiful, clear blue morning, and what had happened in front of the post office had been the most wonderful and exciting event to occur there all summer long. Everyone pretending to read their mail understood the situation perfectly, knew that the Pennys would now really be one of us. The following summer, their house was built at the top of the Big Hill.

The Jog

SIRENS AND FIRE TRUCKS RACING THROUGH THE VILLAGE usually signaled trouble in a familiar place. When the siren went off and the truck turned up our gravel road, we usually assumed that the dump had caught fire again and trotted half a mile to confirm our suspicions and check out what was going on.

The dump caught fire several times during the summer and would smolder dangerously in the clearing. These fires threatened the old maples and pines that circled the area and, if a fire had really gotten going, could have destroyed a number of cottages nearby. By trotting at a measured, steady pace, past the cabbage moths sipping in damp puddles on the road, past the purple harebells and the thimble berries hiding under green umbrellas, one could reach the dump in about ten minutes.

Usually, my friends and I got there just in time to see a lot of smoke and a few small flames, but if the fire were too big to handle, we would, I thought, at least be there to help the volunteers extinguish it. In any case, we could tell everybody where the fire was if they asked. Someone might say, "I wonder why the siren went off this morning," and my friends and I could fill in the details, tell if the fire were big or small, how long it took to put out, and which firemen had worked to quench it. The great thing about trotting, now called jogging, was that it promoted physical endurance.

"Who knows," I thought, "I might have to outdistance the Germans or the Japanese if they invade us." Maybe I'd be needed to carry messages through enemy lines or something, and trotting was exactly how the Indians got information from place to place. Germans certainly couldn't keep up with Indians, and no one would suspect children.

It was damp and rainy one afternoon when the siren went off and the fire truck sped through town. Instead of turning up our gravel road, however, it continued through the village, up the steep hill, and headed toward the state park. A mist hung over the tops of the cedars, the asphalt road was black with moisture, and the heavy smell of wood smoke permeated the air.

Evie and I had never trotted very far from home, but we decided this was an opportunity to test ourselves and started off at a fairly rapid pace. As we reached the bottom of the hill, our lungs and legs were beginning to give out and our trotting became a slow uphill walk instead. Exhausted, and only part-way to the top, we stepped into the road and flagged down an approaching car, assuming the driver was also on his way to whatever it was that was happening in the park. Luckily, the fire was just where he was headed.

Excited with the possibilities of our new adventure, we could hardly wait to get there. A plume of black smoke could be seen rising from somewhere in the woods behind the golf course, not far from the first tee. "That's strange," we said, glancing at each other from either side of the back seat. "There sure are no houses back there. What in the world would burn like that, even in the rain?" The pillar of thick smoke rose wildly above the trees as we approached. Our driver parked his car and we followed him into the brush, tracing the path to the accident by following a fire hose.

In a small burned-out clearing, the charred frame of an airplane rested slightly off the ground, nearly impaled on a number of small trees now reduced by fire to charred spikes. One of the volunteer firemen moved his water hose back and forth over the flaring rubble, though it seemed to do little to dispel the smoke. But as the gray cloud temporarily subsided, I saw something strange in the cockpit. It bobbed back and forth under the pressurized stream of water like a shapeless blackened blob on a tether. My God! It was the pilot, still strapped into his cockpit and burned beyond all recognition.

I stood staring with morbid fascination, questioning if there were something awry in my personality that induced me to kept my eyes fixed on nothing but that scene before me. The thing seemed only a vague embodiment of a human being. Thank goodness Evie and I were in one piece! But, it made one wonder about words like chance, fate, and impermanence.

"What was he thinking when he went down? What must the panic of impending violent death be like?" I thought. I couldn't imagine being burned alive and began to feel sick to my stomach. "His wife, does she know? Was he from around here? Had I ever met him?" Death seemed terribly real, but at the moment it belonged to someone else.

"He'd just taken off from the airport a few minutes ago," a man remarked. "Think he was from Green Bay."

The entire scene was much more than we'd bargained for, and the vision of that black putty-like blob wobbling back and forth in the cockpit was fused into my brain. The rain, the burned trees around the plane, the smell of gasoline, all were sickeningly vivid images on the way home, and they followed me to bed night after night and filled up the room.

No one seemed angry that Evie and I had trotted so far beyond the boundary of the village. "No," I told my aunts, "the fire wasn't at the dump this time." I relayed where I'd been and everything I'd seen, a terrible contrast to summer. Not long afterward, the dump was closed and new cottages were built back in the woods. Besides being a hazard, the dump was no longer adequate for the amount of trash the village generated. I didn't feel bad about it. I guess that was because I'd outgrown trotting after the firetruck, and details about fire could be gotten from Bert at the post office or Bill at the grocery store instead. Bill was a volunteer fireman. Actually, we didn't trot much anymore either, except to get someplace in a hurry. Chasing firetrucks risked the possibility of seeing grisly things.

Volunteer firemen didn't have that great a job, I decided, and although Bill wasn't present at the airplane fire, I never thought of him as a mere grocer again. I wondered how many awful things he'd seen as a volunteer that would never be forgotten. Every time he was on duty and the siren sounded, he had to leave his grocery immediately or else get up in the middle of the night to rush to the scene of an accident. Maybe having lots of things to forget was part of being grown up, but I wasn't ready to try forgetting any more than what I'd already seen.

Cherries

During the post card days of July, cherries ripened. From a distance, orchards on the hillsides were rosy with fruit waiting to be harvested. Mexican pickers arrived in their rattle-trap cars and settled into the rows of one-room shacks orchard owners provided for them. Dark-haired little girls in bright organdy party dresses sometimes appeared in the village, their earrings dangling from beneath their shiny dark hair. During those weeks, storekeepers watched unfamiliar customers closely, as if the town had suddenly been invaded by Gypsies. Mexicans who appeared in places such as gift shops, were viewed by some with suspicion, although I never heard of any actual problems.

These were hard-working, honest people, who lived, though few orchard owners would admit it, in near primitive conditions. Under the circumstances, I was amazed and charmed by their cheerfulness and felt a great deal of sympathy for, and curiosity about, the life they led. Their lack of basic living standards was dismissed by many with the self-deluding conclusion that they really enjoyed their vagabond life and had actually chosen to live that way. Though pressure was mounting all over the country to improve migrant workers' living conditions, there was also truth in many growers' arguments that the season was too short to upgrade housing and still keep the orchards profitable.

Employers could certainly attest to the industry of the Mexican worker. Some families, and they were large, could pick over a hundred pails a day. Mexican adults could pick as many as twenty-five or thirty apiece, but the most I ever picked was thirteen! The price per pail varied according to the season. When cherries were scarce, the growers paid as much as twenty-five cents a pail, but if they were plentiful, it was sometimes as little as ten or twelve cents. The only way to increase a migrant family's income was to have even its smallest members pick.

Hills white with spring blossoming cherry trees were a breathtaking sight. But picking the resultant fruit was tiring and boring work! About 7:00 in the morning, a truck picked up Evie, Grace, and me in front of the hotel and drove us to Irmanetta's Orchard. (Today, those trees have been cut down; gift shops now occupy the space.) At other times, we picked at Grandpa Knudson's orchard owned by Floyd's father. It was located on the crest of the hill behind the village, commanded a superb, broad view of the bay, and usually offered a refreshing breeze that blew beneath an intensely blue Green Bay sky most of the day.

About 8:00 A.M. we picked up our ladders and pails at a central location in the orchard, and it was at that same place we returned to dump our overflowing pails of cherries into large wooden crates and get a drink of water. We were told to pick clean. That meant every decent cherry. We hooked the pails to our belts, adjusted our ladder next to a tree and began from the top. By the middle of the morning, the pails weighed as heavily as bowling balls at our waists, and sticky juice streaked through the black layers of accumulated dirt and tree bark residue from our wrists to our armpits.

After four hours of picking, even our young bones were tired, and the break for lunch was more than welcome! What a relief to stop climbing that ladder, sit on the grass, eat and talk and rest our aching backs. Aunt Mary or Aunt Helen prepared my ample lunches, including sandwiches made with fresh homemade bread, piles of cookies, and vegetable sticks, and after stuffing ourselves and "letting go," it seemed impossible that there were still three or more hours of work remaining. We were more than ready to go home. Thoughts of others swimming in the lake or of the friends we could be playing with, became all-consuming thoughts. But there was no way to get home.

Not wanting to be put to shame by the Mexicans, we geared ourselves for the labor ahead, snapped the pails to our

belts again, and cheered ourselves by trying to calculate our weekly paycheck. Growers, especially Grandpa Knudson, who had the work ethic of the pioneer he was, weren't happy if we took more than an hour for lunch or lollygagged instead of working. We were there to pick, and our activity was monitored by the number of pails we returned to the station, accounted to our name by card and paper punch.

The Mexican workers, on the other hand, swept through the orchard like lightning, finishing a tree and moving on before the three of us had finished half of ours. Children seven or eight years old often picked twenty pails a day. Mothers picked while their babies slept or played under the trees. Occasionally, they stopped to nurse them. Though we began picking near each other in the morning, by afternoon their Spanish chatter could no longer be heard; they were rows beyond us.

Around four o'clock the antique pickup arrived to take us home. We climbed into the weathered flatbed and rode, swaying and steadying ourselves against the makeshift slatted sides. All we could think of was dinner, getting out of dusty clothes, and washing sticky juice from our matted hair. Aunt Helen would have the bath water drawn and cooling. Towels would be laid out and the bath mat down. The house would be filled with the hypnotic aroma of things browning in the oven. "What did you fix for dinner?" I would always ask.

"Surprise, surprise!" Aunt Mary would answer, faking firmness, her eyes twinkling with mischief. "Wait and see, wait and see...."

Aunt Mary was a splendid cook and all three aunties relished building the suspense. No peeking, only guessing. When the platters were finally placed on the table and anticipation had reached its peak, I was glad to have picked cherries all day and to feel completely worthy of that moment. I savored every mouthful, knew I was exceptionally fortunate, and happily, fell into mashed potatoes, calico hash, or leg of lamb with absolute contentment in the candlelight.

Pies

WHEN THE CHERRY SEASON WAS IN FULL SWING AND TONS OF fruit-filled crates made their way by the truckload to the cooperative cannery in Sturgeon Bay, the festival began. It was a festival of pies, cherry cobblers, cherry upside-down cakes, cherry tortes—and their arrival signaled a summer vacation that was half over. Each hotel or restaurant served cherries for dessert, but none that I know of celebrated the season with more orchestrated panache than Anderson Hotel.

In the dining room downstairs, there was an upright piano; the owner, Kitty Valentine, played it. Kitty's husband, a baritone who excelled at show tunes, often entertained guests in the living room upstairs while she accompanied him on the grand piano. Those intimate little afterdinner concerts took place in front of a large living room window. The hotel's location high on the bluff and the wide window allowed a breathtaking evening view of the lake, a jillion stars, and steamer lights on the horizon; it was a special attraction for many guests. The Valentine's love of good music and good food lured many well-known musicians to vacation there throughout the years.

During July, just before dessert was served in the dining room downstairs, song sheets were distributed to all the guests. Everyone participated enthusiastically in singing songs to cherries. Odes to cherries were composed and read. There were pie-eating contests, and every summer there was a new recipe for "cherry something or other." Waitresses wore aprons edged in red with cherries stenciled on the front of them. Kitty Valentine, hotel owner, wore red ribbons and fake cherries in her hair, and pie a la mode and the process of overindulgence became part of the gala summer ritual.

In a circuitous way, I felt a unique connection to the gastronomic revelry such cherry feasts afforded when I participated in those celebrations. The cherries I picked could very easily have ended up in any of those desserts served, and I ate each mouthful of my own dessert feeling that I was part of a chain leading from orchard to cannery. Was I contributing to the enjoyment of pie lovers all over the United States? Was the berry gliding down my throat that moment one I'd personally picked? How many cans did my cherries end up in? Who ate them? Perhaps there was one of mine in nearly every can, in nearly every grocery. They had to be in somebody's can! Maybe on some dusty pantry shelf there is still a can.

At home in wintertime, we selected only cans of cherries from Sturgeon Bay for making pies. The can's wrapper displayed a cluster of dark red cherries on a blue background, and "Sturgeon Bay," was scripted at an angle across the label. I haven't seen those cans for years and doubt if Wisconsin even cans cherries anymore.

Alberta Seiler, employed as chief pie-maker, began rolling out her homemade crusts for Evergreen Beach Hotel about 7:00 in the morning. Until the kitchen was remodeled, they were baked in two large wood stoves and the aroma of simmering coals, simmering cherries, and pastry browning set morning air molecules vibrating. In addition, the appearance and fragrance of pies cooling in the back kitchen was an olfactory event not measurable against any commercial pie today.

I have made few cherry pies in the past twenty years for lack of proper cherries. It would necessitate visiting Door County and bringing them home to freeze. Door County cherries make better pies than those from either Michigan or Oregon. It has to do with the soil. But, the former cherry supplier to the world has since reduced itself to "Pick Your Own" signs along the road or stores where frozen cherries are ordered and shipped like gift boxes of cheese. Tourism is the big business instead. It has taken some of the fun out of pie in July. Furthermore, how is it possible to celebrate pie season sitting in vinyl-covered booths in a mediocre chain restaurant with only one or two friends? Crusts and fillings have to be made from scratch by someone who relishes the competitiveness of trying to make hers or his better than anyone else's. Pies shouldn't be mass produced or sold in cardboard containers in freezer sections of the grocery store either!

Perhaps if it were possible to recreate old hotel cherry celebrations now, they would seem corny. We are used to mass extravaganzas—benefit corn boils with hawkers selling raffle tickets for cars or trips to Disneyland. This was merely a celebratory sharing of harvest and bounty bestowed by a peninsula that one would think had little else to offer except rocks and water. Like irrepressible artistic talent which spills over and inspires others, cherries became a blessing and inspiration to whoever took pleasure in sweets.

A number of years ago when my family revisited Door Country, we returned with a can labeled, “Canned Door County Air.” The words, “Door County” were scripted across the label. Of course, it was a joke. But how wonderful it would have been to have purchased a real can of cherries, bake a pie, and run my finger over the rosy, sweet, sticky goo that bubbles on the edge of latticed pies. I would sing to pies. I would write poems to pies. I would get out my apron with cherries stenciled on the front—and sing!

Connections

By the 1940s, few people stayed at Hillside except oldtimers who had formed sentimental attachments to the place and couldn't imagine vacationing elsewhere. When all the hotels in the village were full, however, the overflow was sometimes directed to Hillside, where guests stayed mostly overnight or until someone checked out from a hotel with better accommodations. The hotel had given up serving meals long ago. Thick paint was peeling from the white pillars of the long, saggy front porch, and the word, HILLSIDE, painted in black on the white siding above the entryway had lost the gloss from its letters. The entire building looked neglected and worn out. Sometimes the owner, Mrs. Olson, rocked on the front porch and her son, Seldon, sat there with her. Most of the time, he perched on the far end of the porch near overgrown lilac bushes that obscured the entrance to a makeshift garage in which he tinkered. Both Seldon and his mother seemed disconnected from regular village life.

I never really got to know Seldon. He was an enigma to me. His expression suggested complete boredom in whatever he happened to be up to, which never seemed to be much.

Though polite and friendly enough when spoken to, he didn't convey enthusiasm about carrying on or initiating conversations. One late afternoon, I saw him sitting near the lilacs. An old crowbar was balanced in his lap and his right foot rested on one knee.

"Hello, Seldon," I said, walking to the porch, confident that I could engage him in meaningful conversation. He had nothing to offer, and I knew so little about him that I had no starting point with which to begin asking him questions about himself, his mother, the other members of his family, or the hotel. I left him, walking on down the road with no more knowledge than I'd had before.

The only time I was inside the hotel was the evening the Moravian Church youth group had a treasure hunt. Every team had a list of things to find and one item was a set of false teeth. Several of us gathered on the side of the road under a street light, checking off what we'd already acquired, and trying to figure out who in the world we knew who might have dentures we could borrow. A mental image of nearly everyone in town flashed through our minds. We recalled each of their smiles, their teeth, and wondered whose were actually real and whose were not. Of course, whoever would lend us some, had to have had them long enough to have acquired a second pair. "Who in their right mind," we conjectured, "is going to hand you the teeth right out of their head?"

"Mrs. Olson! Mrs. Olson!" someone interjected in sudden inspiration. "She's one of the oldest people around."

"Yeh! Yeh!" we agreed. "But who is gonna ask her?"

"Will you?"

"Not me!"

"Well, I sure won't!"

As individuals, we would never have been so bold, but there was courage in our numbers. I knew nothing at all about Mrs. Olson. I had only seen her sitting on the hotel's front porch, and she didn't look like most older ladies I was used to who went to beauty parlors and came back with curly, slightly purple hair. Instead, a thick white mane hung down her neck and over her shoulder and she was partially wrapped in a large plaid wool shawl clutched loosely at her breast.

She was sitting in her living room rocker when we burst in breathlessly and seemed not at all upset by the appearance of four or five children in her living room. "No," she said, she didn't have any false teeth, and unfortunately she had absolutely nothing that was on our list other than a paper clip. (At least that was some help. Paper clips weren't that easy to find in a village where people purposely forgot about organizing.)

I don't recall much of the interior of the hotel, but can easily picture the old woman who was so settled into her chair that it appeared her bones must have grown into it, and the excitement we seemed to have injected into that still living, room where the only sound was a ticking clock. In fact, Mrs. Olson actually appeared to enjoy our interruption and surprised us by joining in the spirit of our game. She suggested we try Mrs. Barnes who lived clear at the other end of the village. We left and ran as fast as we could to reach Mrs. Barnes' house before another team decided that she might a good candidate for teeth and get there before we did. Much to our surprise, she, too, seemed unruffled by our intrusion, went to her kitchen cupboard and handed us her spare pair, and made us solemnly swear to return them the following morning. That dispelled my long-standing impression of her as a total grouch.

Someone told me, although I cannot verify it, that either Mrs. Olson or her daughter, Julia, (whom I never met) was one of the first switchboard operators in our part of the peninsula. She worked out of Edgewater Lodge, the only place where one could go to phone for a dental, doctor, or hair appointment or to make a long-distance call. Sometimes, we sort of wished we had a telephone at our cottage, but after a week without one, we forgot about it and were glad to be so separated. Besides, party lines were common and summer residents had little interest in sharing their private lives with everyone in the village! In the balance between convenience and privacy, privacy won. Long-distance calling was not made easy by the local telephone company, however, which was independent from the larger Bell system.

"I'm sorry, I cannot connect you. Would you repeat that number again, please? I'm not getting Chicago right now." Such interjections were common as we stood on one foot and then the other, waiting endlessly to complete a call. "I'm sorry, all those lines seem to be busy. Would you like to try later? Oh! Wait a minute, hang on, I think I'm getting through now. Hello, hello, is this Chicago? Sturgeon Bay? I'm trying to get through to Chicago. Yes!" Often someone would pick up the phone while we were on it because even some hotels still had party lines. Equipment was poor and when a connection was finally made, the muffled babble of distant callers on a line often made it difficult to hear.

My friends said Mrs.Olson's daughter, Julia, listened in on other people's personal conversations. They knew for sure because in winter things were repeated that couldn't not have been known otherwise, except by listening. Although no one ever said a word, I was told they could hear the clock ticking in the background; no other hotel had a ticking clock that near the phone. Sometimes we'd get on the line and take turns trying to listen for the Olsons listening. We'd say, "Hello there, Mrs. Olson. Do you hear us? Are you getting your earful for today?" There would be no answer, only what we imagined was the faint sound of a ticking clock in someone's lonesome living room.

After the treasure hunt, though, after seeing the old woman sitting in that chair, I felt differently about Mrs. Olson and thought if I were in the shoes of folks living there, I might be tempted to listen, also. The telephone was undoubtedly a substitute for the lack of a social outlet. And why not? In any case, either Mrs. Olson or Julia must have spent many hours on the phone in the past, plugging and unplugging switchboard wires.

The following summer, Seldon sat alone on the front porch. I heard he was trying to sell the hotel but there didn't seem to be any takers. In a couple of years, Seldon was gone, too. "Heart attack," it was said, and, "he used to drink too

much." The clock had stopped ticking. Eventually, the phone service improved—the local company was bought out by Ma Bell and most party lines eliminated. I suppose it depends upon what one calls improvement, though, because there was excitement and something personal and gratifying over hearing an operator struggle to make phone connections, to guard your words when you called home to share your secrets, and to listen for a faint "tick-tock" somewhere on the line.

Seiche

WHATEVER IT IS THAT IS UP OR DOWN OR INSIDE, PLACES THAT cannot be seen or gotten at, are the mysteries that lure men and women to climb, dig, dive into or pull apart. They are the kaleidoscopes we marveled at as children and then dismantled to explore a treasure under glass. The bottom of the lake, however, is an even greater mystery, vast and ancient, keeper of so many secrets.

An underground river was discovered under the peninsula. It ran from one side to the other and its existence might be traced and possibly be proven, I had heard, by use of dyes. If there was a river, I reasoned, then there must be more of them, coursing everywhere, connecting everything, dribbling ancient mysteries bit by bit into one grand soup that was our bay. Looking into the water from a rowboat close to shore, I often wondered what the lake bed could reveal and what exciting treasures might be found. Ancient shipwrecks? Treasure coins?

Somewhere on the coast of Nova Scotia was buried treasure left by Captain Kidd, as I'd read in "The Reader's Digest." He'd left a map, much like the one in Poe's "Gold Bug," and there had been concerted efforts to recover the treasure. It had been buried in a shaft shored up with old timbers, and after Kidd's death, his cohorts had obtained the map, found the Nova Scotia site, and begun digging. They never got it, for the treasure just kept sinking farther in the hole. Nevertheless, the hunt continued, this time by modern treasure hunters in possession of the map, who devised a sophisticated plan to reclaim the box. They, too, failed. A third attempt was made shortly thereafter, involving an even more elaborate stratagem. Parallel and angular shafts were dug alongside the original one, and pumps were used to keep water out and tunnels from collapsing. A great deal of money was raised to execute and continue this final effort, but with the treasure almost in sight, it confounded their attempts and continued sliding deeper into the quicksand-like soil in which it was originally buried.

Seiche was a word occurring frequently in crossword puzzles. "It was a phenomenon on water," Aunt Anne explained, "begun by wind generated by barometric pressure changes and the motion of those wind-driven waves." If conditions were just right, water in a bay gradually receded so that what had once been under water became exposed and dry. It was analogous to a bowl of water. If the bowl was moved, a rippling or sloshing effect began, piling water up on one side of the bowl and then the other. The same thing happens in a lake, although being larger than a bowl and holding so much water, it takes a long time to slosh from one side to the other and recedes at one side for nearly an hour before coming back again. Seiches, I thought, must be rare phenomena, for no one I knew had ever mentioned them, at least not by their proper name.

The afternoon, I saw my first seiche; the sky was cloudy and it looked like rain. I didn't notice it at first but soon discovered that the shoreline looked differently and I ran to the house to tell my aunts about it. They came down to see. The water level was retreating gradually, and I could walk out ten or fifteen feet from the original shoreline without getting wet. Much to my disappointment, however, there was nothing out

there. No flopping fish in puddles. No treasure. Not even an old rusting tin can. Gradually, in less than an hour, the lake returned to its original state, leaving me with the same dreams, questions, and imaginings as before.

No pirate treasure has ever been found in the lakes and no pirates even sailed it, although it is as wild and treacherous as any sea. Captain Kidd's treasure has never been recovered and is, perhaps, still sinking, down, down, down. How far will it go? I can still picture his box, tumbling from some unknown ledge, caught by the currents of some uncharted waterway and then dropped, waiting for another seiche to expose it someplace at the bottom of our bay.

Glimpse of War

"WE'LL SAY, 'HEIL, HEIL', RIGHT IN DER FÜHRER'S FACE," WE sang in rowdy chorus as we stood around the juke box at the ice cream parlor. The "Heils" were punctuated with flatulent, tongue-between-the-lip sounds as we raised our arms in a mock-Nazi salute.

It was a rousing song by which to hate. I imagined myself a German prisoner and wondered if I'd have the nerve to spit like that right in Hitler's face if I were really standing in front of him or if I'd be too chicken. It was so simple at the ice cream parlor. I was thankful not to have the misfortune to have my bravery tested.

Adults had grown weary of it all. It felt as if the never-ending stream of bad news, good news, bad news would go on forever. We pored over the pictures from "Life" magazine in utter disbelief, praying for more brilliant generals and luck to fuel our determination to win and dreading each succeeding graphic issue in the mail. Too many fronts, too many enemies, so long between offensives begun and news of the outcomes. We were nearly dulled to it all. Life, it seemed, had been in such oppressive flux forever, and we were only little actors, playing out our daily routines between conflicting worlds; none of it seemed normal, and all of it was impossible to comprehend. The rationing stamps for sugar, meat, gasoline, and shoes were mere pin-pricking reminders of the desperate situation resulting from wars on several fronts.

In the town of Sturgeon Bay, however, the war had more reality. Sailors were everywhere, buying post cards and souvenirs, and listening to recordings in record store booths. Those were the sorts of random activities young men engaged in who faced uncertain futures.

Mayna and Jackie Avent, additional summer playmates, visited their grandmother, Rose Bradley, during their allotted summer vacation time of approximately two weeks. Because of the large extended family, summers were apportioned, so that everyone who wished to, had an opportunity to enjoy themselves. The Avent's arrival was always anticipated by us girls and their visit always seemed far too brief, though they occasionally could extend their stay or overlap it with a smaller family group for a week or so.

On occasion, Mayna and Jackie's parents brought the Knudson girls and me with them to the city when they shopped. While they accomplished their errands, we swooned over "bell-bottomed trousers, coats of navy blue" and squeezed ourselves into the glass booth of the record store to play the same tune again and again. Something about his "dingy going in and out with the tide." We sang it going home in the car and were told to quit. It was a nasty song, Mayna's mother said. "Where did you ever hear that, anyway?" But the tune was catchy, and we sang it under our breath on the way home.

Mayna's cousin arrived one afternoon at Grandma Rose Bradley's summer house at the top of the big hill. The telegram had just been received. Her husband's submarine had been sunk by the Japanese somewhere in the Pacific. A young daughter stood in somber bewilderment, holding tightly to her mother's hand. Grief suddenly changed the tenor of voices in the house. Grandma Bradley, matriarch to an extended family, was a strong woman and the family gathered to draw from that strength.

Mayna, her sister, and parents had escaped China shortly before the Japanese invaded. Mr. Avent had worked there for The Standard Oil company and Mayna and Jackie, when asked about what China was like, described stepping over dead babies stuffed in paper bags amid the filth of Shanghai streets as they left, an account that certainly stuck in my eleven-year-old mind! The family had been familiarized with tragedy.

Several days after the tragic news had been received, Jackie and I went to her upstairs bedroom, opened the atlas and removed the Ouija Board from the cupboard. Maybe we could discover where the boat went down. We fingered the heart-shaped board over the letters. We closed our eyes. Were we moving it ourselves or was it the result of some dark force?

"It moved! It moved! There. There's the spot! It's got to be!" we whispered. But Ouija Boards changed nothing.

Thereafter, I envisioned periscopes rising in the middle of our bay and Japanese submarines surfacing all over. "They'll come down the St. Lawrence Seaway and take over the whole peninsula," I imagined. "They'll invade the country from the top down instead of from the East Coast and the nation will be completely unprepared." It seemed impossible to envision little Japanese soldiers with guns overrunning the village, shouting and rounding everybody up just as the movies so graphically portrayed them doing in other places they had captured.

Sometimes when the cherry harvest was large and pickers were in short supply, getting to the ripening fruit on time was imperative. German prisoners arrived in large open trucks to work in the orchards. "Might as well make them do something useful," people said. The men waved and shouted at us as they passed and we waved back, although adults told us we weren't supposed to. But, they didn't act like enemies. They looked like us. They looked like anybody's fathers. I wondered about their wives and children? Did their German families know where they were? How did they feel about America, and would they ever get to go back home? My aunts said they were better off here than they would be in Europe and most of them knew it. They were the lucky ones, and I shouldn't feel too sorry for them. Besides, we treated them much better than they treated their prisoners! Nevertheless, it was impossible to see their smiling faces, the friendly waves, and connect them to the horrors in "Life" Magazine.

Suddenly, it was all over and I wondered if I had deserved the sacrifice. There was guilt in being spared, especially in never having to miss loveliness. That summer after the end of The War was a quiet one. The weight pressing on the world so long had left its deep impression, and the collective body was slow to mend. We were recovering from near-death experience, adjusting from darkness into light even in a place which had given so much comfort. This would be a new era and the last of war, we thought. At the same time, we wondered what new path we would be called upon to take in the months ahead. Old songs, suddenly history, were forgotten and replaced by new ones. Submarines were secured permanently to docks and provided jobs for maritime museum guides.

"Now the Day is Over," replaced "The Navy Hymn" at the end of Sunday's Community Sing and "Think of the starving children in Europe," was no longer an admonition to clean one's plate. Aunt Helen purchased the new Chrysler, summer population mushroomed, and gift shops sprang up all over. The pall had lifted, but imperceptibly—I really can't say why—we'd changed forever.

"The Pilgrim"

IT IS DIFFICULT NOT TO BECOME INORDINATELY ATTACHED TO things even though they crowd shelves, require tedious dusting, and can be albatrosses for those who acquire too many of them. Nevertheless, I have discovered that despite my best intentions, for me, the process of detachment is both unnatural and impossible. A case in point is two sets of figurines displayed in my living room secretary. They are mementos, not only of an individual, but of a gift of time; one of those "random acts of kindness" which bumper stickers nowadays exhort us to perform. Is there a possibility we are running out of kindness? Looking at those figurines rekindles images of my brief acquaintance with a gentleman, his boat, and my half hour of glory.

As soon as I saw the ship on the horizon, I knew it was a big one. It appeared to be heading for our bay. "Please, please, dock here," were the words I breathed inwardly and passionately, reeling in my fishing line as fast as I could so as to watch every moment of the boat's approach. This was the largest cruiser I had seen enter the harbor in years. I was awed by the sight of it and concentrated in a telepathic attempt to will it in. Cutting the waves easily, it approached the harbor with the grace of a princess gliding toward her coronation, and I could hardly wait to view her port and starboard sides as well. "Come on, come on!" I urged as it headed toward me and the dock. "I'm going to be here when it ties up," I thought ecstatically. "I get to see what people from a big boat are really like!"

From what I could discern, it wasn't a new boat. The lines weren't right. I guessed it to be at least fifty feet long. The lower part of the hull was a light green, the bridge was large, and the decks spacious. A crewman, smartly dressed in khaki, emerged from the bridge to the side rail as the boat drew close, preparing for the usual docking routine; drop bumpers, heave the painter to the wharf, and see that it was tied securely to the cleats and pilings below.

"I'll grab the painter quickly before anyone else can and secure it," I told myself. "They will be impressed that someone like me can tie a double bowline. And if I do it fast enough," I thought in childish self-delusion, "perhaps they'll hire me. Or, they might invite me on board just to say, 'Thanks!'" But despite such plans I simply couldn't muster enough nerve. Besides, a crewman jumped off quicker than I'd anticipated, fastened the line to the cleat, and reduced me to the ordinary landlubbing gawker that I was.

"The Pilgrim" was from Neenah, Wisconsin, and came and went from Anderson's Dock many times during the latter part of June and July. I fished as often as I could from the big dock just to be seen and to find out everything possible about the owners of the boat. It was surveyed carefully from one end to the other, and my line was set as close to the stern as possible. In short, I allowed them little privacy, and it is a wonder no one ever told me to, go away. Dreams of the possibility of owning, working on, or even marrying someone who owned such a boat became obsessive, like the horse-enamoured girls I knew who whinnied and pawed the ground in equestrian delight.

Mr. Frank Shattuck, the boat's owner, was tall, slender, white haired, had angularly chiseled features, and I thought him rather stern looking. He piqued my curiosity. What sort of job did he have that enabled him to afford such a boat? By asking everyone I thought might know anything about him, I finally discovered he was in the "paper business." Little did I know at the time that he was one of the vice presidents of Kimberly-Clark, involved with more than simply Kleenex.

The grandmotherly Mrs. Shattuck was atypical of the usual yachting crowd. In contrast to some women boaters, who attempted to extend their youth by sporting tans and wearing fashionable vacation clothing, she wore dresses, hosted no cocktail parties that I know of, and certainly didn't put on airs. They were unostentatious and not much different than regular summer residents. Except for the waiting car driven up from Neenah and parked by Anderson's store for their personal use, I thought of them as "our kind of people" and distinguishable only because of a private floating hotel for eating, sleeping, and occasional overnight trips. Each time the boat geared up to go somewhere, I feared they'd left for good and would not be seen again.

During The War, the sixty-two-foot boat had been commandeered by the Coast Guard, a common practice, and completely refitted for surveillance purposes on the Atlantic Coast. It had sailed out of New London, Connecticut, with machine guns on its deck, ready for enemy infiltrators or sneak attacks. Because the war had been over for only a couple of years, "The Pilgrim" had been recently returned and its teakwood decks and appointments restored to their original condition at the owner's expense. That was a patriotic sacrifice and frequent contribution of large boat owners to the cost of war.

By the end of June, I had spent hours hanging around the ship, attempting to converse with the crew, be noticed, and perhaps wheedle an invitation aboard. It was beginning to seem like an exercise in futility. But as "The Pilgrim" returned to its moorings one morning, the crewman threw the rope from the deck to the dock. This time, I grabbed it and tied it to a cleat just as I'd so often planned! Minutes later, Mr. Shattuck appeared on deck. "Hi," I said, trying to be completely casual and convey the idea that ropes and boats were second nature to me.

"Are you the one who did such a good job tying up our boat?" he questioned, looking at me from what seemed a ten-foot vantage point.

"Oh, that was nothin'," I replied lightly, thrilled to be noticed at last. He asked my name and where I lived, and I found myself spilling out everything about the many summers I'd spent in Ephraim, my aunts, how I loved fishing and sailing, and that I was just crazy about boats, especially his. And to let him know I wasn't just any ol' kid with worm dirt under the fingernails and smudges on a shirt, mentioned that I had entered the Yacht Club's 4th of July swimming race.

"That's a coincidence," he replied, "I'm going to be doing some of the judging at their celebrations. What time are you swimming?" I told him. "I'll come down and see how you do," he replied.

Like many who make promises, I thought he was just trying to be nice and never dreamed he would actually show up. He was involved with boats rather than swimming. But, just as another girl and I were waiting for the referee assigned to monitor our race and blow the whistle signaling the start, Mr. Shattuck appeared at the end of the Yacht Club dock. His presence added a new dimension to winning. He had gone out of his way and should be rewarded, I thought, by cheering for me, the winner. There were only two of us; one would be first, one last. I intended to be first.

When the whistle blew, my opponent hit the water ahead of me and took off like a shot. I struggled furiously to catch up. But I was not a disciplined swimmer and had never done any competitive swimming. My right arm pulled much harder than my left and I never sensed that I was aiming far to the right of the finish line. By the time I realized where I was headed and vainly tried to redirect my course, the entire event was over and I was overcome with the shame and humiliation of injured pride and failure. No matter how many swimmers had been in that race, I clearly would have finished last.

"Don't worry about it," Mr. Shattuck said compassionately as he handed me a red ribbon. "You did really well." He patted my shoulder. "By the way, how would you like to go for a boat ride sometime next week—provided the weather is right? Your aunts could come along, too, and I think I could even let you steer the boat."

At home, I was questioned about the race. "Well, how did it go?" Aunt Helen asked.

"Oh, fine!" I told her. "I won second place! I held my ribbon aloft as proof.

"How many were in the race?" she asked.

"Two," I responded, and quickly went upstairs to thumbtack the red ribbon to the wall above my bed, the sounds of their hoots and laughter emanating from below.

Although I knew nothing about it, arrangements were being made with Auntie Waltons for the promised ride. "We're all going out in a boat this afternoon," they announced one morning, and after lunch the four of us piled into the green Chrysler and headed to the dock. It didn't seem possible that it was actually happening at last, and I bounced up and down on the back seat as we drove, my anticipation visually palpable. However, with gray clouds hanging over the bay and waves running high that day, I was fearful it would be too rough and the ride would be put off.

Mr. Shattuck was waiting and warmly welcomed us on board. From that new vantage point, I looked down to the places where I had formerly stood and looked up. In the meantime, he visited with my aunts instead of me, and I wished they hadn't been invited to come along. After all, this was to be *my* experience and I didn't want to share it with adults who always seemed to take over everything.

"Would you like to see the inside of our boat?" he asked us. But, instead of the complete boat tour I'd expected, we were only shown the spacious living room furnished comfortably with draperies and furniture, much in the same style as our own living room at home. It seemed huge, and I imagined what it must be like to carry one's living room around like a nautilus from port to port. I'd hoped to see everything, especially the bathrooms and kitchen, but we were quickly directed to the bridge. The captain explained all the different instruments and then started the engine. "Ger-er-er-er. Ge-ru-er-er-er-rmmm," it grumbled for a moment in that deeply, reverberating, rumbling surge of power characteristic of underwater engines as they catch. But, as we slid slowly away from the pier and the throttle opened, the sound became reassuringly steady. Going north into the waves, we nosed out of the bay.

It was slow going. The sea was rough and though occasional spray and light rain blew across the windshield, I couldn't wait to grab the wheel. "Hold it with me," the captain said, "so you can get a feel of the boat before you take it on your own." He demonstrated the angle to hit the waves, and then, for ten minutes or so, I guided "The Pilgrim" in what I knew would be my only moments at the helm of the ship. This was an experience engineered solely for my benefit, and I was overwhelmed with the generosity of it, knowing it took a great deal of gasoline to operate such a large boat even for a short distance. Five years of expensive fuel and rationing had not yet been erased from memory. From then on, I didn't pester Mr. Shattuck or the boat crew. To the satisfaction of everyone concerned, my craving had been somewhat pacified. Nevertheless, it was still thrilling to see "The Pilgrim" come and go and know that once I had been on board and had steered her.

During the following winters, Mr. Shattuck and I exchanged Christmas cards and letters. Once, he sent me a box of Japanese rice paper stationery. The upper corner of each sheet was decorated with a different handmade water-colored wood block design. I was so excited with the gift that I used only one or two sheets and decided to keep the rest. The box has been in my stationery drawer for almost fifty years, and I still cannot bring myself to use those sheets still remaining. Although Mr. Shattuck's son kept the boat after his father died several years later, I never saw "The Pilgrim" in the area again.

Frank Shattuck's brother, Arthur, had been a noted concert pianist and sailed his own boat when he wasn't on concert tours. After Arthur's death, a number of items from that boat were sold and my aunts purchased several of them. Aunt Anne, being a pianist herself, was taken with two pairs of figurines the artist had acquired in Italy. They were roughly done, much as oil or acrylic paintings executed solely with a palate knife. But that style befitted the ragged old peasant couples represented, their faces expressive of years of toil and deprivation. Dressed in somber period clothing and bent with age, they lean for support on rough walking sticks. Such stoicism and strength of character exudes from the static clay that one can imagine them as major characters in a Grimm fairy tale.

The other purchase was a set of small, circular pottery ash trays with bowls like lotus pools. A Japanese child perched on the edge, leaning back lazily with his arms behind him. His feet dangled in the water and he seemed to be gazing dreamily over the tiny pond. Years later, the figurines and ash trays were given to me as a gift. Aunt Helen felt it was time to do some weeding out and knew how much I admired them. The ash trays have been broken and mended so many times they are beyond repair and the fragments are stored in a plastic bag in the far reaches of my kitchen cupboard. Safely behind the glass doors of the antique secretary in the living room, however, are the figurines. Never could either Mr. Shattuck or I have imagined they would end up where they are or that his memory would be so strongly linked to them. What strange twists, what deeply forged connections.

Mr. Holand and the Fabled Stone

HJALMAR HOLAND'S NAME WAS FAMILIAR IN THE VILLAGE BUT better known to neighbors and those of a scholarly bent. My aunts frequently talked about him and his books in the kind of reverenced tones that indicated he was a very important person. Never having laid eyes on him myself, I paid little attention, though each time we drove past his cabin, my aunts would point it out and voice concern as to how he was doing.

Obviously, he was somewhat of a loner, I thought, one of those creative people whose desire to be by himself was respected by his friends. He was never at a lecture at the Village Hall, never went to church as far as I knew, and never even appeared at the post office. As for his writing, I was too young to have developed a sense of history and so had no concept of the importance of his work. I was aware however, that his book, *Old Peninsula Days* was a kind of historical bible to nearly everyone in the community, and most hotels and cottages had a copy on their book shelves.

The only time I met him was when he invited my aunts and me to visit. They discussed his latest book with him and listened to his account about the accusations that had been made against it, purchased an autographed copy from him before leaving, and took great pleasure in reading it.

Mr. Holand lived in a log cabin about half a mile from the entrance to the Peninsula State Park on the highway leading to the village. It was one of the few original log cabins left in the area, complete with portions of the original white chinking. Large maples surrounded the little place set two hundred feet or so from the road. Inside, the house was furnished simply, but it seemed the walls were being held in place with the tightly stuffed, near-floor-to-ceiling bookcases. Stacks of books, all askew, were scattered helter-skelter about the room.

Short and rather rumpled, the man appeared to have a casual attitude concerning his dress, and he struck me as the typical professor. I sensed, intuitively, that he was a person wearied from some inner struggle, though his intense gaze and manner of speaking projected a fellow with a determined nature and a fighting spirit, characteristic of a Norwegian heritage.

Recalling a brief and somber discussion of his illness, I imagine my aunts were intent upon getting a signed copy of his work while it was possible. They certainly had only a slight acquaintance with him (perhaps because he spent a great deal of time out of the country doing research) but were not ones to let any intellectual opportunity pass them by. Not until years later, after reading his book *Westward From Vinland* concerning Viking explorations in North America, however, did I have any real understanding of what the scholarly portion of Mr. Holand's struggle was about.

Except for those who have intense interest in the Kensington Stone unearthed in a farmer's field in Kensington, Minnesota, in 1898, few have likely ever heard of Hjalmar Holand. It was his accidental involvement with the remarkable stone that diverted his interest from English literature and history to Viking exploration, sparked his research, and eventually led him to decipher the runic marks carved on the rune stone. If the authenticity of the Kensington Stone were to be proven, a good portion of North American history would have to be revised. But lacking a degree in Norse history and runic writing was a circumstance that unfortunately, worked against Mr. Holand in the end.

Archeologists had had evidence of a Viking settlement on the Atlantic coast. But then Viking axes and other paraphernalia were unearthed in Canada; Marquette, Michigan; Bismark and Minot, North Dakota; and in Thief River Falls, Minnesota. Those artifacts and the runic stone itself, along with thousands of other clues, convinced Mr. Holand that the rune stone was authentic and that the Vikings had indeed sailed through Hudson Bay and traversed the Red River.

Most tantalizing were the watercolors and descriptions by

American artist George Catlin, who, in the early 1830s, spent two years with the Mandan Indians and found striking similarities in their physical features, beliefs, and way of life to those of the white man. But Mr. Holand's adversaries were unwilling to accept the scholarship of one trained in English literature and history rather than runeology and were highly protective of their own professional reputations. As it turned out, they were quite capable of skullduggery, also. Not long after Mr. Holand's book was published, which comprised nearly a lifetime of dedicated research, they had set out to discredit him. The *Encyclopedia Britannica* eventually described the Kensington Stone as a forgery, a hoax in the same league as the Cardiff Giant, a money-making scheme devised by George Hull of New York state in 1869. (In order to prove the myth that giants once lived on earth, he had a huge stone statue carved, buried, and later "exhumed". Both Hull and P.T. Barnum profited from a gullible public.) The original rune stone, considered for a time as one of the greatest archeological discoveries in North America, was returned from the Smithsonian in Washington, D.C., to a small museum in Alexandria, Minnesota.

The controversy concerning the stone's authenticity will likely continue, though someday perhaps there may be revelations about runic writing and new discoveries of Viking artifacts that will rekindle interest in Mr. Holand's research. I was fortunate to have met a man who worked so hard to present historic truth, but less fortunate to have met a man so spitefully used and discredited. Thankfully, and as with a host of others, however, Mr. Holand was in love with Door County. So much so in fact, that it is his exciting and beloved early book, *Old Peninsula Days*, first published in 1925, that to this day gives Door County aficionados a detailed and spellbinding history of the peninsula from Pére Marquette, Indians, and early settlers to tourism and cherry orchards. Hjalmar Holand's gift to Wisconsin and his community has, in turn, given him a prominence that, until new evidence surfaces about Norse exploration in America, will be sufficient and enduring.

Hair

My aunts took me to the beauty parlor to cut off my hair. I hated the new look with a passion. I wanted mine long. Deborah, who sat in front of me in seventh grade, had long, reddish golden hair. Straight and smooth to her shoulder, it curved under gently and perfectly all the way around, and then rose along the angle of her chin. When she leaned over her paper to write, the hair fell forward softly, and I couldn't keep from marveling at it. In addition, Deborah had the figure for pleated wool skirts and looked better in them than most of us did. Her seat was flatter and the pleats didn't poke out in the wrong places when she stood. Under her crewneck Shetland sweaters she wore white, round-collared dickeys or a simple strand of pearls. The style complemented her hair-do and gave her an air of sophisticated innocence. She was a combination of an alluring Esther Williams in a swim suit (a movie star known for her choreographed swimming), and a sweet, rufflely aproned wife demonstrating the joy of Sunbeam Mixers in a magazine ad. Yes, her hair style was exactly what I wanted.

I was short. My red and green checked skirt poked out front and back in the wrong places, and my profile was disgusting. Each time I saw the reflection of myself in the window near my desk in English class, I became more miserable. "I hate it, I hate it, I hate it!," I snarled through clenched teeth when I came home from school and confirmed the horrid profile in the large mirror in the living room. Then I'd pound my rear end fiercely, and with a final "I hate it," deliver the hardest whack of all. But it was no use. No fat was beaten away. The new green summer slacks with baggy seat and pleated front Mother purchased for me didn't help things either. "Perhaps," I desperately hoped, "perfectly styled, long red hair like Deborah's might make me more attractive."

After school was out, Mother drove me up north for the summer. At first, Auntie Waltons said little about my hair, but soon they were dropping hints about what I could do to improve it. Eventually, they told me I looked like a cocker spaniel and Aunt Mary said she just couldn't stand looking at it any more. "Either get it cut or we'll have to send you back home," they teased, and although I wasn't sure they really meant it, nevertheless, acquiesced just to be on the safe side.

In my eyes, the new haircut made me look fat, short, and very unsophisticated. It had no style, hung straight, and ended somewhere around my ears. Viewing myself each morning in the bathroom mirror only intensified self loathing. It took most of that summer for me regain even partial self-confidence about my appearance.

By the next summer, I was a little thinner and arrived in June with hair only to the shoulder, and in deference to my aunts, pinned it back with barrettes so I wouldn't be accused of looking like a dog again. The hair wouldn't curl under as it was supposed to, however, despite my rolling it up in socks and sleeping with white wads around my neck all night. I could never get it to look like Deborah's. In addition, swimming twice a day took out the curl, so I protected what little was left by using a swimming cap and trying not to get my hair wet.

Swimming presented a second problem with self-confidence. I didn't fill out the front of bathing suits at all and falsies weren't yet fashionable. "Perhaps, if I sew my Jr. Lifesaving badge on the upper right thigh of my 'Catalina,' swimsuit" I reasoned, "eyes might see the badge and not bother to look for breasts." If that didn't work, I hoped having my red hair long and ravishing might do the trick.

Still, I stayed in the water while others sunned on the beach, not wanting to expose my many physical deficiencies. I chose a ridiculous, flowered wraparound house dress, more suitable for my mother, for walking home from the beach instead of a tight-fitting T-shirt like everybody else. The dress had a ruffle of eyelet lace around the neck and down the front and bloused voluminously on top, camouflaging I thought, what I didn't have. I tossed my head back to flick hair from my face like other girls who wore theirs long. It was a movement meant to be casual and said, "This hair is such a bother, always in my way, and there are so many other important things to think about." It was an gesture meant to attract attention, though nobody seemed to care.

Tom was one of the boys I thought I liked a lot. A cousin to two of my best friends, he appeared one summer when it was his family's turn to vacation at his grandmother's summer house. He was a good deal older than I, making him doubly attractive. Sometimes, a bunch of us joined with his cousins on family picnics, and once I got to ride in the car with him and the son of Presidential Candidate Adlai Stevenson. It certainly wasn't a date, but I told everyone at home it was. And, I imagined what it would be like if Tom discovered I was the one he loved despite my age and said he'd wait for me to grow up. I could quit school and spend summers with him at his cabin for the rest of my life, and then my good friends, Mayna and Jackie, would end up being relatives. That dream didn't persist for long, though, because he had a lot of cousins and everyone only got a two-week stay at the Bradley cottage. I needed much more time than that to win his heart!

In my summer scrapbook, pictures were labeled: "Mayna and Me," "Tom Throwing Water at Me," "Evie, Tom, and

Me," "Joyce and Me At Jackie's Birthday with Tom." I practiced during my long-hair-stage, trying to look sexy. Pointing my toes as I raced into the water might make me seem taller, thinner, and more glamorous and model-like, I thought. I cocked my head so drifting hair covered my freckles and glasses and wondered if I would ever grow up to be as sensual as screen star Greta Garbo.

It was a painful period in which the only relief was to give up, put on old clothes and go fishing, or sailing, or something! I hated my hair, my figure, my freckles, my glasses and my braces. And I had to admit that my aunts were right, after all. I did look like a cocker spaniel! Somehow, I wasn't able to acquire the right look or pull even part of it together, and I wondered if I ever could. Girls seem to today, even the flat-chested ones.

The only job my friends and I had was picking cherries. The money we made wasn't enough to buy any clothes, so our parents chose and purchased them. Our sexuality was imagined and unpracticed and wouldn't come naturally for a few more years. In the meantime, we were ungainly, pretentious, giggling Cinderellas, wishing for a prince to carry us away. By the end of my middleteens, the decision to have my hair cut again was my own and everyone breathed a heavy sigh of relief. "You have no idea how ridiculous you looked," my aunts said several years later, shaking their heads and smiling. "But you've turned into a lovely young lady after all."

It's hard to live with what you've got at age fourteen, but eventually one has to come to terms with it. I talked myself into believing adolescent misery was making me a better person if only to make myself feel better. Certainly, early physical perfection would have been dangerous! It was good to have time for a lot of fishing and a lot of thinking, to see myself reflected in the water while watching perch nibbling at the line below, and to decide all on my own that, long hair was really not my style. Deborah moved and who really wanted to look like Greta Garbo anyway?

The Dedication

MOST PROTESTANT CHURCH GOERS WERE MORAVIANS, AT least in summer. The Lutheran minister preached more fire and brimstone than most summer people were accustomed to. Aunt Anne frequently played the organ at the Moravian Church, and on warm Sunday mornings music and singing drifted from the open doors and windows of the little church set against the hillside along the upper road. Its steeple was visible from most places in the village.

Many summer residents even belonged to the Ladies Aid; organized fundraisers, bazaars, art fairs; and donated stunning bouquets from their gardens for the altar. This country church gave people a grounding for the summer and was often more important to them than their church back home. In part, that may have been because of the magnificent view of the bay from the church entrance, the steeple framed in the evening moonlight from the upper road, or the uncomplicated country-like interior, but beyond that, credit had to be given to the messengers, Rev. Weingarth, and his successor, Rev. Westphal.

Both were charismatic men. They had an intensity about them that demanded respect, and their sermons were delivered with such power and sincerity that it was impossible to be unaffected by them. They were dedicated evangelists who reflected a true calling, and their messages of love, service, and the good news of God in Christ were a perfect complement to our summer nirvana.

My aunts insisted that I attend Bible school there the first spring I stayed with them. It gave them a couple of hours free from child care. I thoroughly resisted and resented any possibility of indoctrination.

"Anyhow," Aunt Mary said, "it won't hurt you a bit and possibly could do you a lot of good. You're going." Though they seldom attended church back home, we barely missed a Sunday service in Ephraim. Initially irritated with their demand that I accompany them, I must say the social aspect of being there and the sea of flowered hats around me provided a great deal of entertainment. Soon I extended the "hand of friendship" to my neighbor with the enthusiasm of a regular member.

Rev. Weingarth organized and directed a youth group that often attracted ten to fifteen teenagers from the village. Families encouraged children to participate as an alternative to hanging around the ice cream parlor in the evening and to add a wholesome focus to their vacation. With a few exceptions, it was the same group every summer, and we had great fun going on treasure hunts, having picnics, singing around bonfires, and getting reacquainted after winter separations.

The favorite and most inspirational picnic site was not far from the entrance to the Peninsula State Park. It was accessible only by a long flight of wooden steps leading straight down from the top of the bluff to the huge, smooth, limestone table below. The perimeter of the ledge was protected from the sheer and dizzying drop-off by a railing which most of us tried to avoid getting close to. Perfect for our use because of its privacy, Rev. Weingarth frequently selected it for our meetings.

By the time darkness settled over the bluffs, the hot dogs had disappeared and the last of the marshmallows had flamed, dripped, and oozed in crisp, sickeningly sweet sufficiency. Sparks drifted into the blackness, at last submitting themselves to the distant river of the Milky Way. Running lights blinked methodically as freighters inched along the horizon and places in the village on the opposite bluff suddenly became identifiable; the post office, the church steeple, Wilson's Ice Cream Parlor. Sometimes, I thought I could see the lights of our own living room.

At last it was time for Rev. Weingarth to present his sermonette. But first, he added another log to the fire and divided us into groups. We sang rounds, and sent lyrics like "White coral bells, upon a slender stalk, Lilies of the Valley deck my garden walk," out over the cliff and into the night.

Then he would stand, a tall, slim silhouette against fire and darkness, and speak of the joys of Christian service and tell stories of Moravian missionaries.

"We must carry the Christian message home with us," he said, "for we are called upon to live the Word in everyday life. It won't always be so easy as tonight in this beautiful place." We ended the service with, "We are climbing Jacob's ladder, soldiers of the Cross," the music and words so compelling that I flushed with the shame of a child unappreciative of so many good fortunes.

It was at that moment that I secretly promised to become a missionary when I grew up, and go to Africa or South America to serve the Lord, defying crocodiles, tsetse flies and piranhas. Certainly God wouldn't allow me to be eaten because there was so much work to do, and I would prove to be an invaluable servant. I tried to forget those martyrs whose faith hadn't saved them from being boiled in oil. "But if I were a missionary," I questioned sadly, "would I ever be able to come back here? Maybe," I reasoned, "I can do something just as important close to home." But then I felt inwardly ashamed to have made such a selfish, half-hearted commitment in the face of all my God-given gifts. One was supposed to give her or his all!

How many of us were touched by those evenings together and carried the words, the fervor, and the fire into later life is a question. It would be interesting to know. But, without a doubt, we were the better for the experience. Those splendid nights, the friendship, the surroundings, and the cross we had joyously been called to carry, merged into an inseparable whole. After church on Sundays when we shook Rev. Weingarth's hand and looked him in the eye, we were reminded of his expectations, and I doubt if any of us has ever been the same.

Night of the "Half Moon"

IT WAS EVENING WHEN THE WIND BEGAN TO BLOW HARD OVER the water and the rain tore across it in great, gray sheets, blotting out what little was left to be seen anywhere. I went to bed that night immersed in wildness and relishing the fury of it all. The next day, it continued to blow. Waves curled, crested, and crashed on the sand throughout the afternoon, and white froth piled up along the edge of the shore.

Sometime during the morning, disconcerting rumors were heard at the post office and the grocery store. A yacht had gone down! At first, it was suspected to be the "Utopia," one of the newest large sailing vessels on the lake, owned by Mr. Peterson from Peterson Boatworks in Sturgeon Bay. Bits of news filtered in all day, confusing, for none of it was known to be at all accurate; and a feeling of foreboding and sadness cast a pall over usual daily activities. All stories were conflicting.

First, only one girl and her friend had made it to shore. Then it was said that the mother had swum to shore and had seen the girls go down. Later reports said only a pet dog on the boat survived, and finally, it was reported the dog had drowned. But, by the end of the next day a more complete picture of the tragedy was available and the name of the boat was confirmed. It was the "Half Moon," a sloop purchased from Jimmy Roosevelt, son of President Roosevelt, by Leathem Smith of the Leathem Smith Shipyard. Mr. Smith had been on board that evening in 1946 along with two other men, (one of whom didn't accompany the group out to sail) his teenage daughter Patsy, and one of her friends. Out of the four people on board, Mr. Smith's daughter, who, fortunately, was an excellent swimmer, was the only survivor.

She reported that she and her friend, Mary, had swum approximately fourteen miles from where the ship went down in heavy seas. Just as her feet touched shore, she reported, she turned around and shouted to Mary that they were safe at last. But her friend was gone. "If only they'd had a radio," people in the village said, shaking their heads in disbelief. "If they'd had one, they never would have started out from Marinette at all." Perhaps. But alterations to the ship, its cockpit and bulkhead, had made it a death trap under circumstances of freak waves and squalls.

That evening, I walked down the hill to the beach. It had begun to clear in the northwest and the sky at the horizon was a pale yellow and wind-streaked with heavy dark gray clouds. It continued to blow steadily, and waves rolled in long deep swells to the shore, the spray shooting up and spewing through the air as angry water crashed against docks and exploded over breakwaters. I imagined myself struggling to swim out there, bucking waves, treading water, trying to rest and to gain my strength in the cold, uncertain dark. I shivered at a scenario too close for comfort, for I'd always dreamed of sailing on boats like the "Half Moon." On clear evenings, I could see the twinkling lights of Marinette and Menominee miles away on the other side of Green Bay, the place from where the ship had sailed that fateful night. "She could have gone down near here," I thought and imagined the "Half Moon" sinking just outside our bay.

Perching on a large rock and staring at the determined

swells and the darkening sky, I recalled my own past encounters with the power of the lake. Just off the shore from Cana Island and its lighthouse on the Michigan side of the peninsula, the hull of a wrecked and rusting freighter had protruded from the water for as long as I could remember. It had run aground and broken apart against rocks a few hundred feet off the bouldered shore.

Access to the lighthouse was easy during the years when the lake level was low. In fact, my aunts and I had picnicked there. At that time, anyone could walk to Cana Island over the rocks that formed a little causeway and linked it to the mainland. When a friend of mine was old enough to drive, the two of us went to Cana Island one afternoon to explore the lighthouse on our own. This time, however, the water was considerably higher and covered the causeway stones. It was the only approach to the island, so we picked our way carefully, trying to place our feet on rocks that gave us the broadest purchase. Though we didn't suspect it, the swells circling the island came together over the rocks, and as they met and retreated, created a significant undertow.

About halfway to the island, the water was up to our knees and the pull on them so strong we were barely able to keep our balance on the unstable, slimy stones. It was as if the lake were determined to get us, like someone urging, "Come on. Come on!" and emphasizing impatience with us by tugging at our shorts and shirt sleeves. Terrified with the prospect of being sucked into the drop-off on either side of us, we debated whether we should go ahead or attempt turning around on the slippery stones. But by continuing, we faced the possibility that the water might become deeper which certainly increased our risk. And once on the island, we would have to brave it back to the mainland again. So, we turned around gingerly and, with trepidation, made our way back to shore, aware that at any moment we could stumble fully clothed into the water and be sucked away.

Each summer, I spent a week with a hometown chum,

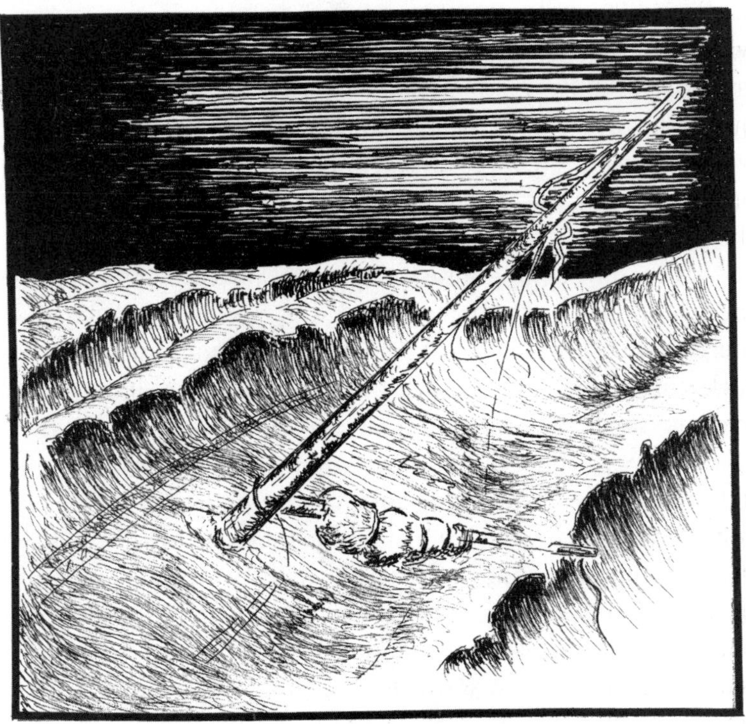

Anne, her sister, brother, and her grandmother in the little village of Valmy north of Sturgeon Bay. White sandy beaches and a different lifestyle on the Lake Michigan side of the peninsula provided a happy change for a few days.

In return, my aunts invited her to spend a week with me. The arrangement allowed each of our families a little reprieve. When the water wasn't too cold for swimming, we dove off the Glidden Lodge dock near her grandmother's cottage. The water there was absolutely crystal clear and its depth deceptive. Even at fifteen feet or more, the white grains of sand below appeared to be individually distinguishable and the bottom no more than an arm's length away. Sunlight and water had created a giant magnifying glass. No matter how deeply we dove, we were never able to get anywhere near the bottom. For a moment, I imagined drowning there, lying on the bottom on my back, face up, my body, and especially my eyes, appearing twice their size to those who peered down at me through the water from the edge of the dock. Everyone was trying to reach in and pluck me out, but it was too deep. In a sudden rush of terror, I stopped diving, left the dock and ran home. After that, I swam closer to the shore, making certain that my toes could always touch the sand.

Sometimes, I played and swam from a friend's raft anchored in our bay. The water was rough the afternoon I dove off alone and swam under the raft to explore its underside. The barrels beneath moved and rocked as the thing tilted wildly with the waves, and my foot unexpectedly wedged tightly between them. For what seemed a lifetime, I struggled to free that foot, certain my lungs were going to burst, that I'd never make it to the surface, and that I would be found that evening dead on the shore, just as the child who'd drowned there earlier in the year.

All these recollections were focused around the sinking of the "Half Moon." Taken together, they were a dreadful collection of images linked to a lake with a monstrous appetite. Completely unpredictable, its ever-changing landscape was nevertheless compelling and enticing. But, it was a master at deception and lured one to complacency. The lake was angry that evening when I sat on the rocks and contemplated the tragic accident and the hundreds who had succumbed to the will of squalls and waves over the years. It was enough to set one thinking about the vicissitudes of life and the meaning of pleasure. I wondered. Was there a quota which the lake demanded? Had I cheated it and the price extracted by someone else for me? It was a gloomy, pagan thought, but it was a personification I wasn't equipped to dismiss. Something in the deep, hard swells beckons like a friend and has never ceased tugging at my arm.

The Car

AUNT HELEN DIDN'T WANT MOTHER TO SEE THE CAR. SHE said it would be too upsetting. Mother saw it anyway, and it was upsetting. She had come for one of her brief visits and was greeted by Aunt Helen standing next to the stone wall above the parking area, Aunt Mary at the bottom of the stone steps, and Aunt Anne by the screen door. "Well, Nell, we have a problem here we can no longer handle," was the greeting she received even before she had a chance to shut the car door and remove her suitcase.

"What are you talking about?" Mother questioned in surprise as she stood in the driveway, her hand still grasping the top of the door frame. The tone of her voice indicated she had already switched into the defensive mode common to mothers under siege. "What in God's name is the matter?"

"Corinne has been in an accident," Aunt Helen replied sternly, her lips set tight.

"Oh, come on in, Nell," Aunt Anne added apologetically, always one to attempt mediation in awkward situations, "we've plenty of time to talk it over." I knew that would entail talk about my violating trust and hanging out in bars.

From an adult viewpoint, I had been a "bad girl." But, as far as behavior went, I wasn't much different from anybody else my age; certainly somewhat headstrong, though certainly more naive. It was an awful age for most parents to endure. Fortunately, most of us survived, some of us barely so, and trouble almost always involved cars or liquor. On the other hand, I wasn't so bad as Carol, the most defiant of all summer friends who lived down the road with her grandmother. By pleading, threatening, and brow beating, Carol made her grandmother's life such hell that she finally capitulated to Carol's wishes out of sheer desperation. Thus, Carol got to use her granny's car whenever she wanted and was able to wheedle her way into doing anything she set her mind on. "No," meant nothing to her. Carol was what one would call, "out of control."

There were never such disagreements with my aunts, who trusted me implicitly and who wouldn't have stood for such behavior in the first place, especially from a fifteen-year-old. I would have been whisked home. Nevertheless, both Carol and I ended up in accidents. Her granny's Nash, which appeared solid enough to survive an encounter with even the meanest of Mack trucks, met its demise hung up on a large rock pile a few feet off the road in the Peninsula State Park. She lost control while air planing at full speed over her favorite roller coaster road, which induced a sensation paralleling the sudden acceleration of an elevator. But before the car was terminally gutted, we sometimes piled into it after we were tired of swimming and drove with her to a small beer bar between Fish Creek and Ephraim to dance and show off in our swim suits, though I still wasn't thrilled over how I fit in mine. There seemed to be safety in numbers. My aunts never suspected.

The more sophisticated, older crowd hung out evenings at "The Rock," which offered entertainment along with booze. Its big attraction was a New Orleans jazz band imported from Chicago. The band was really good and really loud, so loud in fact that as kids drove by, the sound alone tempted them to stop and join the throng. On Friday nights, the place was jammed with what at the time was a new phenomenon: kids and cars.

Hotel waitresses, whose parents would likely have disapproved had they known, lived it up on their night off, and young men, bored with the confinement of a family vacation, prowled for excitement. Around midnight, a string of fifty or sixty kids led by a Pied Piper trumpet player, kicked and snaked their way out the back door of the rustic stone bar. Clasping the waist of the person in front of them, they wound in centipede fashion through the parking lot, around the front of the building and returned through the back door.

"Roll out the barrel, we'll have a barrel of fun," everybody sang at the top of his or her lungs, then fell breathlessly into chairs and quickly ordered another round of beer. 'The Rock's reputation drew young people from all over the peninsula, and I dreamed of being able to go there some day. Instead, it was the little bar further up the road where we girls sometimes went in the afternoon that became our substitute.

"The Parkway" was where I met Lonnie, a nice guy despite the name. I'd never known a boy with a name like that. It sounded funny, as if it had been lifted from a paperback southern novel whose cover showed ladies in antebellum dress, posing in arbors dripping with wisteria. Lonnie was in his Army uniform each time I'd met him and that gave me a good feeling. After all, the Army stood for truthfulness and honor, and they were supposed to help people. In addition, he acted like a gentleman. He visited and danced with us when there was no one else who did so.

During the summer, the Knudson girls lived above the hotel laundry, an old wooden building with sleeping rooms upstairs. It was private, furnished with old beds, hand-tied quilts, and calico drapes that substituted for closet doors. The large hook and eye on the inside bedroom door was the final touch to a room with the cozy intimacy of a club house. There, we could stay up as late as we pleased, talk about anything without being overheard, and be as silly as we wanted, so long as we didn't disturb guests. I loved spending time there, and whenever I asked Floyd or Laurel if I could sleep over with the girls, they almost always said, "Yes," and my aunts usually agreed. They believed I was safe there, would stay where I said I was going to be and that a fifteen-year-old couldn't get into too much trouble. But one evening when the girls had dates, I decided I wanted to do something, too, and asked Joyce's boyfriend to drop me off at "The Parkway." They could pick me up on their way home.

It wasn't an exciting evening there by myself. I felt out of place, bored, and had drunk more than enough Coca-Cola. As the hours dragged on, it became obvious my friends had forgotten all about picking me up and that I'd have to figure out a way to get back to the hotel another way. Lonnie was the only person there I knew and I pleaded with him to drive me. "I've got to go." I told him. "If my aunts ever find out I've been here, they'll really kill me! Please, can't you give me a ride?"

"But, I'm not really ready to go yet," he answered. "Maybe someone else can."

"Yea," I said, "but I don't know anybody else. Come on. Please?" I kept pestering.

"You better be careful," the bartender warned when Lonnie went to the other end of the room to shove another quarter in the juke box. "The guy's been drinkin' beer in here off and on all day."

"Gosh," I answered, "he sure doesn't act like it." Anyhow, I thought, its only beer, and if he'd really had that much to drink, I'd certainly be able to tell. So what was the alternative? I sure couldn't walk home! Lonnie finally said, "Yes," and I felt a huge load had been lifted off my shoulders.

He drove slowly and I relaxed. I was thankful he was a reliable friend and that I had proven to be such a good judge of character. I really could handle problems on my own after all.

But in a moment it was over. I was instant tumbleweed in the front seat as the car suddenly hit gravel at the sharp, flat curve of the road. A brief vision of the shattered windshield spun before my eyes and then nothing, until I woke up in the grass alongside of the road far from the car. Did I dare try standing up? Was my face all right? After a few dazed moments, Lonnie and I discovered we were both in one piece, a real miracle after I caught sight of the car's condition in the moonlight. From apparently having skidded on its side, the passenger door was scraped and badly smashed. Somehow the car had managed to right itself.

Though shaken and bloody, my first fear was that someone had heard the car skid and phoned for an ambulance. Not only would everyone in the village find out how bad a person I was, a policeman would awaken Auntie Waltons in the middle of the night. They would be terrified and Aunt Helen beside herself. I envisioned her driving to the Sturgeon Bay hospital to pick me up. I imagined being the cause of her second heart attack. The first one had occurred before I could remember. Fortunately, there were no sirens, and on inspection, the car looked drivable. We crept ten miles an hour into town, praying all the way that the radiator would last until we reached Dr. Sneeberger's house near Wilson's Ice Cream Parlor.

Dr. Sneeberger had been the village doctor for years, but it was rumored that he was finally thinking of retiring. He had frequently said that, at his age, he was sick and tired of being dragged out in the middle of the night to patch up accident victims and deliver babies. By the time we arrived at his house, it was early morning and the village was pitch dark. After ten or fifteen knocks on his door we could hear feet padding across a floor and saw the light flip on in the living room. "I'm coming, I'm coming," a frustrated, muffled voice called. He was just sticking his left arm into the sleeve of his robe as he opened the door.

"Damn fool kids," he exclaimed when he saw us, "when are ya ever goin' ta learn! I've seen enough of this stuff. Drinking I suppose?" And then with a sigh added, "Well, come on in. I'll have to patch you up."

He turned on the light in the small office next to his living room and got out his antiseptics, swabs, and bandages from a cabinet against the wall. "Well, you were just damned lucky," he said with a bit more compassion as he sat us down and cleaned the gravel from our cuts and washed the blood from our faces. Bandaging the worst spots, he kept repeating, "Just damned lucky! Just damned lucky."

"How much do we owe ya?" Lonnie asked when he was finished, "'cause all I've got is a couple of dollars." I didn't have money either! We glanced at each other. It was bad enough being in such an embarrassing position, but not having money to pay him seemed worse. "We'll have to pay you later," we told him sheepishly. He said that was all right; the only thing he wanted was to go back to bed and try to get some sleep.

"Hope you've learned your lesson," he remarked as he closed the door. Lonnie dropped me off at the hotel, where I spent what was left of the night with the girls and tried to figure out how I was going to explain the bandages when I got home.

There was no possible way to avoid the truth when I appeared with dressings on my arms and face. Auntie Waltons looked stunned the moment they saw me. "What in the world happened to you?" Aunt Helen questioned in a voice indicating she feared the answer. I felt totally rotten as my aunts listened quietly to my story, not saying much of anything. They didn't raise their voices or tell me how terrible I was. They didn't have to. They just very firmly set their jaws.

"I'm sorry," I told them in desperate tones, unable to raise my head enough to meet their judgmental gaze. "I really am. I'll never do it again, I promise! Don't you believe me? Talk to me. Say something! I know how mad you must be. I don't blame you. But really, I promise. I'll never do it again."

"I don't think you're going to get the chance to, young lady," Aunt Mary replied impassively, rising from her chair and disappearing into the kitchen. And, that was the end of it. Nothing more was said. Conversation around the house was limited to essentials as far as I was concerned. Aunt Helen went to see the car which had ended up at the junk yard and paid Dr. Sneeberger. Lonnie vanished.

When Mother came, I had to repeat the entire story again, and my tenuous situation at my aunts became a reality when they told Mother they couldn't take responsibility for me anymore. "Teen-age years are just too difficult, Nell," they stated. "These days, with cars and alcohol and accidents," they continued, turning to me as they said it, "we just don't think three old-maid aunties are up to it. Especially when we can't trust her anymore." Of course, Mother was embarrassed and ashamed. I had failed her. And after all she'd done to make me turn out right! She didn't know how much I felt I'd failed everyone I ever knew!

"Get upstairs and put your things together," Mother ordered, and later in the upstairs bedroom whispered firmly, "We're getting out of here tomorrow."

When my aunts found out we were leaving so soon, they begged Mother to stay. "Please, Nell," they pleaded, "you don't have to go. This is ridiculous! Don't let this incident spoil your vacation. Certainly, you can stay out this week!"

"No, I think it's time," Mother replied. "I'm going home where I can sort this all out."

The next day, she got up early and packed the car. We had told the Oshkoshers goodbye the night before. They understood both sides but didn't give me much sympathy, which wasn't much of a surprise.

"When you betray one you betray all," I thought.

"I do wish you'd reconsider and stay, Nell," all three aunts kept saying as we awkwardly downed our final breakfast with them for the summer. Now I felt responsible for spoiling a life-long friendship in addition to ruining everybody's summer, and I wondered what people in the village would say about me when they understood the reason I had gone home.

All three aunties stood in the same places they had stood when Mother had first arrived. I kissed Aunt Helen and Aunt Anne goodbye tearfully and told them again how sorry I was. Aunt Mary came last. She was more strict than the other two, and I always felt she had the least sense of humor for and understanding of children. I was too young to catch the twinkling eyes that betrayed her apparent seriousness, nor did I understand the wry tongue-in-cheek remarks she often made.

"I'm growing up now," I told her defiantly, "and I want to do the things other kids do. If you weren't so strict all the time... You just don't understand kids my age." Aunt Mary looked me squarely in the eye, and never one to allow me the last word, laughed gently in poised self-confidence, her chin raised in her own defiance as she stood at the head of the driveway near the car.

"Someday, you'll understand your old aunties!" she shot back. Her face was flushed with hurt and anger. I might as well have slapped her. Then I recalled the special things she'd done for or given to me: mittens knitted and clothes sewn when I was small, the deviled eggs she knew I loved, the homemade bread with jam, the sandwiches so carefully prepared and wrapped, desserts made, and a litany of other never-ending favors throughout the years. "Maybe God will strike me dead during the drive home," I thought.

"But we still love you," added Aunt Helen, this time with tears welling in her eyes.

"You bet we do," Aunt Anne chimed in, her eyes wet, too. Aunt Mary nodded solemnly.

We waved goodbye like always, but things were different than they'd ever been before and I knew they would never be quite the same again.

The tension between peer pressure and adult expectations in new and uncertain times was difficult. Drive-in theaters and bars all catered to the post-war freedom of youth. That freedom involved cars and caused many parents to think twice about the joys of long family vacations. Increasingly, the curves and hills of the peninsula became scenes of weekend crashes. Daredevil boys who lived to tell about their exploits related their survival stories like proud war veterans and were stupid enough to repeat their folly a couple of weeks later. One fellow wrecked his parents' car twice, as well as those they subsequently, foolishly, bought him.

What would my summers be like from then on? That was too depressing to contemplate. Even if my aunts let me visit for a week or two, it just wouldn't be enough. What about my friends, and fishing, and poker with the Oshkoshers? Maybe I'd never see any of them again!

School started in September and I kept dreading the following uncertain summer ahead. Then in October, Mother suddenly announced that she just had to get away all by herself. "I think I'd like to see what Door County is like in the fall," she said.

About the middle of the week, she called home, pretending she just wanted to find out how my stepfather and I were getting along. "By the way," she mentioned as casually as she was able, "you'll never guess what I've done!"

"What? What did you do?" we both asked from separate phones, expecting a rather ordinary answer.

"Well, she replied proudly, "I've bought a cabin. The first time I saw it, I knew it was absolutely perfect. It's just like a doll house! Cute as a bug's ear. It has a tiny loft overlooking a big living room and a wonderful fireplace with bookcases on either side. Both of you will love it. And guess what?"

"What?" we said, hardly daring to believe what we'd just heard.

"We can move in next spring!"

The Disbelievers

THERE WERE JUST A FEW UNPLEASANT OCCURRENCES DURING all my summers, and one was not of my own making. It was an experience not atypical for a sixteen-year-old then or now and a reminder that even in the best of worlds, nothing is all sweetness and light, human nature being what it is. Even though what you are about to read is on the dark side and might seem inconsistent with the rest of what I've previously chronicled, not including it would be a disingenuous portrayal of the process of growing up.

You see, at one time I'd admired him, this acquaintance of so many years. Suddenly however, he had become repulsive, and I couldn't understand why I felt that way, except that he no longer was the person I'd known a year or so earlier. When our conversation began, everything felt as normal as it had always been. He thanked me for being nice enough to stop in at his office for a visit and pulled out an extra chair for me to sit in. "You have no idea how wonderful it is to have somebody to talk to," he said, leaning back in his chair with fingers locked behind his head, and I was glad that I'd followed up on my inclination to drop in and say, "Hi."

For a couple of minutes we 'caught up with each others' lives and exchanged small talk. "You know, Gretta is well, frigid." (I sensed a strange tension between my shoulders.) "Oh, don't get me wrong, I still love her, but we don't have much in common anymore. We're all talked out and she's too busy with the children."

I was flattered that an adult thought I was finally mature enough to be confided in though not certain I really understood how the word "frigid" related to one's wife. A feeling of uneasiness came over me. Maybe I was reading him all wrong though. If so, and I probably was, I didn't want to be rude by saying the wrong thing, or insult him by getting up and leaving.

"The girl I really wanted married someone else," he went on. "And you know, I never even kissed her? I certainly had plenty of opportunity! Just didn't take advantage of it, I guess." He leaned back in his chair and eyed me intently. His face appeared flushed and his nostrils were slightly flared. "My, you're really growing up. You're certainly not the little girl I used to know! Do you still like to fish?"

"Yea," I answered with hesitation, wondering where the question was leading. He had to have seen me going to and from the dock nearly every day, tackle box in one hand and fishing pole over my shoulder! Of course, he knew I liked to fish!

"Well, then, why don't we go fishing together some time? Or better yet, maybe we could go over to my other property and just lie on a blanket and look at the moon. Just that. That would be all. How does that sound?" He paused, watched me squirm, and waited for my answer. "Well?"

"Well what?" I answered, pretending not to understand his question and trying to change the subject.

"Wouldn't you like that?"

"You mean fishing? I like fishing best of all," I told him, figuring that was the most innocuous reply. And what reason would he have to even think I'd want to lie on a blanket with him anyway? Even to a slow learner, his intent now seemed pretty clear. I couldn't believe what was happening and wished I could run away.

"Well," I told him in as casual a voice as possible, "guess I'd better be getting home." I got up from the chair.

"Now, don't go telling anyone about our conversation," he cautioned softly, leaning toward me. "You know how gossipy small towns can be. Why, just the other day, I gave a friend a ride in my truck and she looked all over to see if anyone was looking before she got in." He chuckled. "Now, isn't that silly? So this is just between you and me, 'cause other people wouldn't understand at all." He paused, giving me one of those funny looks again. "I'll get in touch with you when the time is right. You promise not to tell, now?"

"I promise," I replied feeling sort of ashamed. This wasn't the kind of conversation I'd want to tell to anybody! "Don't worry about me. I won't tell." I was a little frightened by now. He'd seemed peeved when I'd said I'd rather fish than lie on a blanket, his face flushing as it had earlier. So, I didn't care what I said, just as long as I could get out of there fast, without making him angry.

I walked home in a daze, and although I thought hard about it, just couldn't bring myself to tell Mother or my aunts about the conversation. "Maybe it's all my fault and I said something wrong," I conjectured. I felt sullied and betrayed and, at the same time, guilty that I'd participated in such an episode. "But, what could I have said that was so bad?" I couldn't think of anything, and even though I tried hard to put that afternoon out of my mind, I simply couldn't do it.

"Wanna ride?" Gretta hollered good naturedly from the open window of her truck several days later. I was walking to the post office. She slowed and pulled up beside me. "Looks like you're headed in my direction."

I didn't know what to do. Maybe she was suspicious! Had he told her something, like our conversation had been my fault? Maybe she was trying to trick me so she could find out more. But, I if ignored her, she'd be sure to wonder why. Unable to sort out the situation, I hopped in, thinking normal behavior might allay any doubts she possibly had.

"We never see you anymore," she chided as I settled into the seat. Remember how much time you spent visiting with us when you were growing up? You should come over soon and see us again. Why, the kids have grown so much, I'll bet you'd hardly recognize them. We all miss you, you know." I thanked her for the ride and waved goodbye. Now I felt worse than ever, smothered in the shame and guilt I didn't deserve, and totally overwhelmed by it.

During the following month, I came face to face with my tormentor at church. He was the usher greeting everybody at the conclusion of the service, and I slithered by him on the outside of the line while my aunts smiled, gushed, and shook his hand. I tried to ignore him without being obvious. But several days later as I stood in line at the post office, there he was again, this time behind me. Suddenly, I felt a hand touch mine, then grab and squeeze it. I felt all sick inside. "I'll let you know when the opportunity is right," he whispered, knowing I would say nothing in front of all those people. My hand felt "ishy" when he let go, and I wished there was someplace to wash it off. I also thought more seriously about telling Mother. But, before I got up the gumption or even had the opportunity to do so, he appeared at the door of the antique shop where I had a part-time job.

It was a stormy Friday evening and I was about to lock the door, hop on my bike, and head for home. I couldn't believe it when I saw him peering through the screen and hung on to it tightly so he wouldn't be tempted to open it. He'd brought his two children with him, each one clasping a hand.

"I just came to tell you that the time is right," he said with a grin, the excitement evident in his expression despite the screen and dull outside light, "and sooner than I'd thought! Gretta's in Indianapolis. Come to my house when you're through here, and we'll watch movies or something. I'll put the kids to bed."

In our last encounter, he'd protected himself and ensured my silence through the people around us. This time he'd used his own children as cover, and his boldness seemed more menacing. Adrenaline kicked in. My heart was thumping wildly. I knew I had to say something so he wouldn't dare bother me again, even at the risk of making him furious. Nevertheless, I certainly didn't want his children to suspect anything was out of the ordinary. What would they tell their mother when she returned? "Daddy asked a girl to come watch movies with him while you were gone," they might say. Then, Gretta would ask them all kinds of questions, discover who the girl was, and I would be blamed.

Speaking with my teeth clenched, a smile on my face, and in as normal a voice as possible, I hissed, "How dare you bring your children here! They should be home in bed. You know, I used to think you were nice, but you've spoiled everything. And you're old enough to be my grandfather!" I slammed the shop door in his face and worried about turning off the light, getting on my bike, and then riding home in the dark. He could be out there somewhere, waiting for me. For a moment, I contemplated sleeping all night in the locked shop. But, without a phone at our cottage, there was no way to talk to Mother or even to ask her to come and pick me up.

"Don't you dare tell a soul," she warned when I told her the entire sordid story. "Trust me on this one. I can tell you right now, no one would believe you! He's too well liked. People would just say you were a young girl fantasizing and had made up the whole thing. That's always what happens. Rest assured, you aren't the first one he's done this to! I always thought there was something sneaky about him. Never did trust him." I bristled. How infuriating. How unfair that girls are the ones who get blamed and men get away with everything. Why would people assume girls are the liars?

Mother and I keep the secret almost until the end of summer, until, that is, she just couldn't take it any more. My aunts constantly exclaimed about what a wonderful a person he was. "Isn't he wonderful? Gretta is certainly a lucky woman. Don't you think so, Nell?" they'd repeat time after time, expecting Mother to agree and rave about the scumbag. "And to think of all he's done for us! He's just a godsend!"

"Such a good Christian," Aunt Anne added in emphasis, nodding with her typical pious look. I could tell by the expression on Mother's face that she was about ready to explode.

"No, I don't!" she finally blurted, "I think he's a G.D. hypocrite!" Then she told them everything, and just as she'd predicted, they didn't believe a word of it. They acted totally shocked that Mother believed my story and insisted I had made the whole thing up.

"Well, even if he did say those things, Corinne certainly must have egged him on. Somehow she must have," one of my aunts emphasized reproachfully. “Because he just isn’t the kind of man who could ever do things like that.” Finally, they stated in no uncertain terms that it was nothing but a nasty story and that none of it should ever even be repeated. Ever!

“Boy, how I wished they’d seen his red face and the wild look in his eye,” I thought, furious over their denial. “Then they’d believe me!” In actual fact, my aunts were more naive than I had ever been, and I wondered how they’d survived unscathed for so many years. I could understand men sticking up for men, but these were women who should have known better. Worst of all, if they couldn’t believe me, almost their own flesh and blood, certainly no one else would.

Even with Mother’s bolstering, it took a long time for my feelings of complicity to fade, and at times I still wondered if it had been all my fault. Young girls lacking self-confidence are easy prey; wolves pick on weak sheep. I’ve always wondered, too, if some people aren’t born with a genetic tendency to be more naive than others. It is a trait that can get one into trouble, and gullibility is a flaw I’ve never quite been able to overcome, even though I’ve conscientiously tried.

A couple of weeks after my aunts had heard and rejected the story and emotions had calmed a bit, I managed to put some finality to my experience. One night, I tossed another log into the fireplace and took savage pleasure watching the spider I’d seen crawling on it scurry over the smoldering bark, suddenly stop, explode, and finally disappear. Though it certainly didn’t change anything, I felt better and was thankful I had become a little wiser.

That summer signaled the end of blind trust in men, but it left an empty space where that trust had once been. It was a void quickly filled with questions about human nature and, for saftey’s sake, they would be reflected against the face of every man from that time on.

Abandoned House

EXPLORING WAS PART OF SUMMER, AND BEING ABLE TO DRIVE the car alone on occasion allowed a much broader range of wandering. At each opportunity possible, sketch pad, watercolors, and jar of water on the seat beside me, I drove down every unfrequented back road and abandoned trail in hopes of discovering something I had not seen before. It had been a quiet day of rain and mist. But late in the afternoon, the gray lifted. Overwhelmed with cabin fever, the smell of wet wild grass and the promise of sun and late afternoon shadow, I was drawn like a Gypsy to the road.

For miles, I had the narrow blacktop to myself and, on a whim, turned north. Suddenly, there it was, a house whose mottled, gray, wet siding was drying unevenly in the western light of late afternoon. I parked the car and stood there, looking, sensing there was too much to see and to explore. Painting would have to wait until another day. There was no breeze, no sound, only a resounding mesmerizing emptiness filled with questions.

Why had they gone away? Who was the last to shut the door, and when? Was it too many springs of clearing stones upon stones upon stones from the rocky ground? Had it been a happy house with children, or one of worn bent bones and aged forgetfulness? Was death the ending of it all? Or debt? Or flight to warm January sun, far south?

The chinking still looked strong between the weathered logs, the wooden shingles on the upper half still well aligned, though curled. The old glass windows that distort one's view had not been shattered. But, the house had seen its day and somehow said that it was tired. Darkness through the windows up and down spoke of it. The field of daisies undisturbed around it, the old brown porcelain door knob told the tale. Rocks from the land delineated the adjacent field, the house in the center, and the maples squaring three sides, framed it. Best of show! If I could, I would have left the gravel road facing the house and walked close in to see; looked through those windows for the signs of life—old shoes, a kitchen spoon, torn curtains on the floor, mattress or frame of iron bed. But I could not trample on the field of daisies, growing like weeds on old graves.

Nothing to do but stand there staring, painting the canvas of memory. What is it about old barns, decaying silos and the rusting plow that stirs us? What is it about vacancy that draws us to know more? Silence. So much of it there. Questions. All that is unknown about tomorrow mirrored there.

Charlie

EVERYBODY KNEW CHARLIE STREGE. HIS CONTRIBUTION TO the village was local color. Frequently, he and his horse, Silver, were seen tearing through town at breakneck speed. Charlie's white hair was stripped straight back like the tail of his horse, and the sides of his red-and-black wool shirt followed suit. I marveled at him often as he leaned close to his horse's mane in the mindless abandonment of a dead-run, at one with the animal and the wind and aware of nothing but those breathless, exhilarating moments. Perhaps his wild racing substituted for the blur of booze which often plagued him in his younger days, or perhaps it momentarily blotted out the numerous personal failures that separated him from other men. But I imagine it was more out of pure joy—the irresponsibility of childhood he'd never left behind.

His fading gray farmhouse was barely visible from the road at the top of the hill above the village. It was surrounded by old maples and overrun with shouting children for whom he was never fully able to provide. On pay days around suppertime, the sound of argumentative, angry voices could be heard even at our house—two fields, a road, and many trees away. It was common knowledge that Charlie drank up his money and brought little of it home.

Mrs. Strege was always busy and pregnant, leaving no energy for children other than her own. The only time I ever saw her was when curiosity and adventure lured me to spy on her house. As I crouched in the underbrush, the screen door opened, slamming against the clapboards, and two young barefoot children emerged with their mother in pursuit. Ignoring her calls, they circled the maples, hands fingering the rough gray bark, whooping and giggling as she tried to catch them. Instead of siding with children against adults as I was prone to do, I felt sorry for the woman who appeared so tired, worn, and demoralized; she was helpless in corralling any of them. Though drawn to discover more about the children in tattered overalls and their mother in her drab gray dress, I crept away, fearful that I might be noticed and that some gray spirit might rub off on the remainder of my summer.

Near the end of vacation, the fighting stopped. Mrs. Strege had cancer, and Bonnie, who was close to my age of ten or eleven at the time, assumed responsibility for the family. "Poor Mrs. Strege," people remarked, and "Poor Bonnie. She's so young!" And finally, when it was over, "Poor woman, at least now she's got some peace." Bonnie, who used to play with us occasionally, suddenly could hardly get away, her childhood slipping by while the rest of us swam and picnicked. How the family managed, if one could even call it that, was due in part to collective village concern and the fact that Charlie had at last become a little more responsible.

It wasn't that Charlie didn't have dreams or ambitions. He did. But he simply never seemed able to prolong his luck long enough or accumulate the resources needed to carry them out. Several summers after his wife died he worked at a nearby stable and then acquired a few horses of his own. Winter boarding costs were high, as was insurance, if indeed he had any. Knowing that and the difficulty he had just putting food on his own table, it was a mystery to everyone how any in the family survived. Despite those problems, he guided a string of tourists on horseback along the main road several times a week. His personal appearance was rag tag, as he dressed only for the ride and not for show. But when he mounted Silver, he acquired a stature and dignity he didn't normally display.

If one wanted to ride more impressive horses, the stable at the south end of the village near the golf course was the one to patronize. But nobody ever received a better ride than when they went with Charlie. Though some derisively called his horses nags, they were nevertheless dependable—never rearing, bolting, or rubbing their riders off on trees. Best of all, Charlie let his horses trot, whereas other stables were more cautious. He would appear with the horses at the end of a road near one of the hotels to meet his group. There, they would mount and travel back roads instead of trails, bird watching and visiting along the way, taking longer than the usual hour.

To my surprise, I was not forbidden to ride with Charlie. Although his roughness certainly didn't cast him in the common mold of men, my aunts decided getting to know him wouldn't be harmful and might, in fact broaden my experience. He was a

likable fellow, and riding with a group seemed perfectly harmless.

I saved my quarters. This expensive sport wasn't within my budget, though he charged less than regular stables. "Maybe," I told Charlie, "I can help you. Like be your assistant or something. I just love riding. I promise I won't be any trouble. Please? Can I? Please?"

In the end, my persistence must have won him over, for when his rides weren't all booked and I had tired of fishing, he let me ride even though I couldn't pay his full fee. On the trail, he expounded on his dreams, his bravado spilling out in entertaining anecdotal conversation as we rode. Next year, he'd have an assistant. Next year, the horses would be better. When everyone returned next year, he would have his own stable.

He related impressive stories about how hard he worked in the shipyards and the things men tell each other to define their competence and masculinity. But the summer after my first year in high school, Charlie didn't appear. I was told he'd been forced to sell his horses that winter and was cleaning stalls for someone five or six miles away. I got directions and set out in the car to find him.

He had changed. "They took them all," he said, "all except my Silver. Nobody'll ever get that one. No sir!" He seemed surprised that I had cared enough to track him down. Sometimes, he was too busy shoveling horse manure to ride with me and instead let me take Silver out alone. It wasn't much fun riding by myself, but it was the only way to perpetuate our relationship and the pretense that circumstances had never changed. A need to discover what made him tick was undoubtedly partial motivation for my seeking him out; the lure of something unexplored. But I don't think I ever came even close to understanding him. Our roots were too divergent. Charlie had to be accepted strictly on face value. "Take care now," he'd caution, "'cause if ya don't come back in half an hour, I'll have ta come lookin' for ya.'"

Along the wooded path where I rode alone, large maples and saplings grew close to the sides of the narrow trail, which twisted through a quiet sea of sun-washed green. Tree trunks and branches were black with forest moisture and mottled with lacy gray-and-yellow fungus swatches. At last, the trail breathed outward into an open meadow near the barn.

Though nearly twenty, Silver had lost little of his spirit and was still sure-footed and sensitive to the needs of his rider. Trusting, I relaxed, allowing him to trot unguided along the narrow path while I enjoyed the heady odor of warm woods and the brush of maple leaves against my cheek. A casual glance ahead, however, alerted me to immediate danger. Held part-way in its fall by other trees around it, a large maple lay angled, rider high across the path. Silver could pass under it, but I doubted if we both could make it. Instinctively, I pressed my body against his back and prayed while the hairs on my head tangled and caught in the tree bark, fractions of an inch above.

Another afternoon I found myself lying between Silver's feet after he lost his footing on rocks and soft mud at a curve in the slippery trail. He stopped immediately as I slid from the saddle to the ground and waited for me to mount again.

One would imagine that such narrow escapes would have been enough to put me off, but they were not. It is a marvel that most of us reach adulthood at all, and the extent to which odds favor our survival continues to be a mystery. Certainly, no one beyond the age of ten is unable to recall similar incidents, which, in retrospect, make the blood run cold. Such was the case when Charlie and I raced the horses in a dead-run to the barn, ignoring the real possibility of mishaps that could have brought tragedy to either one of us in that hummocked, stone-strewn field.

Farmland on the peninsula contained as much rock as soil, and winter frost forced stones upward year after year. In fact, they were so numerous that farmers were unable to plow until they were removed and accumulated into the piles or the rock fences that defined most fields. Charlie and I had ridden the horses over the broad meadow that faced the barn before. It seemed smooth enough, and we raced the horses to the barn side by side, hypnotized by our speed, eight pounding hooves, and the high-pitched vibrations of wind in our ears. I did it alone frequently, returning again and again to the sprinting point to repeat the ride without thought of gopher holes, rocks or missteps until years later. Those incidents I didn't share at home for fear a stop would be put to my riding. As chilling as those experiences were in retrospect, I still cherish them like a badge of honor.

By the time I was in college, Bonnie had moved to Chicago and even the younger children had disappeared. On a damp, chilly afternoon in fall, Charlie and I rode aimlessly, crossing to the other side of the peninsula, exploring roads and discovering new scenery. Knowing it would be a long ride home, we stopped to rest at a rundown, wooden roadside tavern.

The bar was filled with back-bent farmers in dirty, well-worn overalls. They perched on stools along the varnished bar, gulping beer, shaking leather dice cups, and slapping wrinkled fists on tables with each roll. We had one beer and left. Charlie had not been tempted to drink more as I'd feared he might, and we returned to our cabin to sit on the back steps and rest awhile. We fed the horses green apples from the tree beside the door and nursed our aching bones.

That was the last I saw of Charlie. Silver died that winter, and by the following summer, Charlie was gone, too. I missed him. I missed what was uncomplicated and straightforward about him—his simple childishness, his lack of pretense. Perhaps missing infers some sort of understanding. He had not been a good father or husband, and he lacked many of the qualities needed for so-called success in life. Still, there was something to be envied about him, and what he added to village life was worth more than a thousand post cards and more memorable than all the pictorial sweatshirts now sold in local gift shops. He was a part of the whole of our community which we accepted in it entirety.

Now, Charlie would be out of place on the main street of town. The horses would be a danger to tourists crowding the streets to shop, searching for that perfect Christmas gift, or musing over a possibly romantic and exciting weekend ahead. His hair would be too disheveled, the smell of horse too strong, and his clothes too soiled to be respectable. He would be asked to race, not through town, but on some back road above the hill, away from the main road by the post office where no one would become uncomfortable with the magnificent imperfection that gave him life.

Epilogue

OUR NEWLY PURCHASED COTTAGE WAS CLOSE TO MY FRIENDS at the hotel and to my aunt's house also. So, for the following twelve years, summer remained very much the same except that Auntie Waltons and the Oshkoshers frequently came to our house for dinner and poker for a change. No one ever mentioned the accident either, but my indulgent stepfather, Ray Dickerson, sometimes drove me to "The Rock" on Saturday nights, told me to have fun, and graciously faded into the background. He, too, grew to love Ephraim as much as the rest of us, and after so many years without a man in the house, we operated as a regular family again. But over the succeeding years, Aunt Mary died, then Aunt Anne, and then my stepfather. Instead of teaching school for the rest of my life and spending summers ever after in Ephraim as I'd dreamed, I married a man I had met at the Peninsula Music Festival. His job wasn't even in the state!

The ceremony took place in a tiny Episcopal church in Fish Creek, four or five miles away. Aunt Helen paid for my wedding dress which was made by Bill Crum, a local clothing designer and tailor for the few summer residents who could afford him. Floyd, my much-loved summer father, gave me away, and the Knudson girls were maids of honor. Laurel prepared food for the reception, and most of the village attended. It was a memorable community event but one that heralded many changes.

When we left Door County after the honeymoon, driving down Highway 57 as I had done for so many years, I couldn't keep from crying. Blinking through my tears, I knew it was the end of all the gravel roads of childhood. The future was filled with questions, and I wondered for a time if getting married had been the right decision. If things could just go on the way they were forever!

As is often the way with family summer homes, a heart-wrenching reality eventually has to be faced; the time to sell. Both Aunt Helen and Mother, alone by then and in their eighties, contacted a realtor, and by the following spring, two new families began building memories of their own in the places where I had for so many years accumulated mine. After the closing, I stuffed things which I wanted to keep from the cottage into the car. It would be a long trip to St. Paul. Surveying the still wonderful empty room, the yard, and the tree outside in which I'd carved my initials, I sighed and told myself that it was high time to grow up. "You might as well face it. Those days are gone forever."

Of course, time turns everything to memories; that's what the remainder of our lives are built upon. Still, nowhere is it written that just because one grows up they can't still be children. Children are more fun anyway. And, so long as one continues to give away the delight, the wonder, and the excitement, such as I'd been given by an entire village—and its very special people, things can be much as they always were, even in a different time and place. For as long as one wills it, asphalt roads can end and the gravel roads of childhood still endure.